WISDOM & WEALTH

WISDOM & WEALTH

A CHRISTIAN'S GUIDE TO MANAGING YOUR LIFE AND FINANCES

GREG WOMACK

BEACON HILL PRESS
OF KANSAS CITY

ISBN-13: 978-0-8341-2321-2
ISBN-10: 0-8341-2321-5

Printed in the
United States of America

Cover Design: J.R. Caines
Interior Design: Sharon Page

Library of Congress Cataloging-in-Publication Data

Womack, Greg, 1963-
    Wisdom and wealth : a Christian's guide to managing your life and finances / Greg Womack.
      p. cm.
    ISBN-13: 978-0-8341-2321-2 (pbk.)
    ISBN-10: 0-8341-2321-5 (pbk.)
    1. Vocation—Christianity. 2. Money—Biblical teaching. 3. Wealth—Biblical teaching. I. Title.

    BV4740.W66 2007
    241'.68—dc22

                                    2007024302

10 9 8 7 6 5 4 3 2 1

Contents

Introduction

My 12-year-old daughter, Raegan, and I were on our way to church one Sunday when she noticed some people stepping out of a new, foreign sedan looking like they belonged in an issue of *Vogue*.

"Dad, are those people wealthy?" she asked.

She has asked me that question a lot lately, especially when she sees indicators of riches. I try to explain that wealth is relative. For example, a person with a well-paying job who drives a newer car and lives in a nice house might be considered rich to someone who doesn't have those things, but that person might look at a neighbor who has more and wish he or she was as well off.

My idea of a wealthy person is one who could stop working and go anywhere and do anything he or she wanted without running out of money. That's quite a bit different from folks who earn six-figure incomes but couldn't survive if they quit working.

Our society puts a high priority on having it all. And we are a blessed society. America boasts more millionaires than any other country with, according to the Spectrem Group, 8.3 million households worth a million dollars or more.

But many of these people are unfulfilled. While incomes have doubled over the last 50 years, research shows that people are not happier. When someone earns enough to meet basic needs, additional income barely affects overall happiness. We are status-conscious creatures, always comparing ourselves to others; always striving for more, thinking it will provide a sense of accomplishment and satisfaction. Many middle-class Americans sacrifice their futures to appear wealthy.

How can you build and maintain the wealth you need to sustain you and help you accomplish your life goals? Is it possible to have wealth and be fulfilled? For centuries people have sought the answers to these questions.

You don't have to look far to see that many have sold their souls pursuing fortune, power, and fame. How many famous people who supposedly had it all lost it? Most had prominence and all the money they could spend, but their money could not buy peace and fulfillment. This problem is in every industry and facet of our culture.

Money and your attitude toward it will either destroy you or help you fulfill your dreams. True success is not based on your net worth. It comes when you realize life means more than money and possessions, and you are living your purpose and passion for life in helping others.

We do need money to live, but without wisdom, money will leave you unfulfilled and always craving more. Wisdom will allow you to use money to achieve joy and fulfillment.

What if you discovered proven secrets on how to find and manage wealth without losing your soul? With this information you could establish a blueprint to make wise money decisions and learn how to use money to accomplish your life's goals. This information would help you balance your money and your faith and help you understand that you can have it all no matter your net worth. What would you be willing to do or pay to obtain this treasure of wisdom and knowledge?

In this book you can learn timeless principles from the Bible and Solomon's wisdom that you can apply in today's planning. This book can help you get a handle on your finances and plan for a brighter future. You will learn from my 20 years of helping people manage their money and plan their estates. I'll share some of the successes and mistakes I've seen people make. You may recognize many of the concepts and ideas in this book—most of them have been around for a long time, but hopefully you will see them in a different light as they relate to your life. I will help you understand how to control money instead of letting money control you.

This book is not about how to pick hot investments or time the markets. However, it will show you how to use the time-tested wisdom of Solomon and biblical principles to develop a financial blueprint—from managing debt to investing your money and creating a legacy.

More importantly, this book will help you work toward your life purpose and show you how to use money as a tool to enhance your journey. Join me on this journey as we seek advice and wisdom from the Oracle of Jerusalem, King Solomon. Many of these concepts can help you fine-tune your life purpose and money plan, but you will never find peace by following formulas.

Some people miss a secret that's right in front of them and shouts for them to listen and take its advice. This secret has been around for thousands of years and is continually relevant. It is Wisdom.

Without wisdom your money and your life will have limited effect. Applying the Bible's wisdom and principles will help you develop a successful life strategy that will benefit not only you and your family but also your community and the causes you care about. To use money to help fulfill your life's purpose you must develop a plan and put money in its proper place. This book will give you the ideas and tools to start developing your plan.

I encourage you to go through this book with a partner. This will help each of you move forward with your plans and provide support and accountability. So let's get started.

The Oracle of Jerusalem

Americans spend millions of dollars every year on self-help books on ways to make fortunes: how to buy real estate with no money down, how to buy stocks and other securities, how to make money from home, just to name a few. Recently, I saw where a California businessman won the highest bid for $500,100 to dine with one of the wealthiest men on earth—Warren Buffett. Mr. Buffett is also known by the nickname the Oracle of Omaha. [Oracle: a person giving wise or authoritative decisions or opinions.] Buffett, from Omaha, Nebraska, is the second wealthiest person alive, right behind Bill Gates, cofounder of Microsoft Corporation. Buffett's estimated net worth is $52 billion. *That's a millionaire 52,000 times over!* Despite his immense wealth, Buffett is famous for his unpretentious and frugal lifestyle. He continues to live in the same house in Omaha he bought in 1958 for $31,500, although he also owns a summer house in Laguna Beach, California. His annual salary from his company Berkshire Hathaway is $100,000, nominal by the standards of senior executive compensation in the United States. The Oracle of Omaha is sought out by those who wish to increase their wealth by learning his management style and investment philosophies. Many wealthy people are also following his example of charitable giving. In June 2006, he made the commitment to give away 85 percent of his fortune, approximately $31 billion dollars, over a period of years, most of which would be going to the Bill and Melinda Gates Foundation. Buffett's donation was the largest act of charitable giving in United States history.

You may not be able to afford dinner with the Oracle of Omaha. You may not even be able to hire a financial coach or counselor, but if you're like most Americans, you could use some guidance and wise counsel on planning your life and your finances. While there have been many wise and wealthy people throughout history whose ideas and accomplishments have come and gone, there is one person whose wisdom and business knowledge has stood the test of time for more than 3,000 years. This wise sage of the Middle East was known throughout the world long before printed newspaper and cable television. His words of wisdom and recorded experiences still provide the needed direction and advice for one's work, relationship with money, possessions, and purpose in life. Thousands of years ago, ancient kings came from the far corners of the earth to seek the wisdom and knowledge of the person I refer to as the Oracle of Jerusalem. This sage of the Middle East had such knowledge and wisdom that kings paid thousands of pounds of gold, silver, jewels, horses, and spices in exchange for his secrets and wisdom, every year.

The oracle I'm speaking about is King Solomon. The Bible tells us that Solomon was the wisest and richest person who has ever lived. It would be hard to try to determine the total amount of his worth in today's dollars. His gold collection alone would have been worth over $80 billion in today's money. The Bible tells us that kings and queens of the earth paid tribute to Solomon every year of his reign at the rate of 25 tons per year. Solomon was the author of 3,000 proverbs and wrote 1,005 songs. The Books of Ecclesiastes, Song of Songs, and parts of the Book of Proverbs are ascribed to him. The story of Solomon is found in the Bible starting in 1 Kings, chapters 1—11, and in

2 Chronicles, chapters 1—9. The name *Solomon* means "peace/welfare." Many of his teachings and wise sayings are recorded in the Bible and are still relevant today.

1

The Solomon Factor
What's Your Treasure?

Wisdom is better when it's paired with money,
Especially if you get both while you're still living.
Double protection: wisdom and wealth!
Plus this bonus: Wisdom energizes its owner.

—Solomon *(Eccles. 7:12, TM)*

IN THE BOX OFFICE HIT *Indiana Jones and the Raiders of the Lost Ark,* Indy, a renowned archaeologist, was on a mission to find one of the world's most valuable items: the ark of the covenant, the chest holding the Ten Commandments. Indiana began a treasure hunt to find this greater-than-life artifact before the Nazis could.

Life can be an adventure with alluring opportunities for success, fame, and fortune. Just like Indiana Jones, many people today frantically chase their dreams and the mighty dollar hoping to find their treasure—peace, happiness, and fulfillment. And when some arrive at their destination, they discover their treasure wasn't worth the time and price paid.

Seeking happiness and success, some parents work two or three jobs to make ends meet. They try to claw out of the financial mess they've created, neglecting precious time with their young families. They don't realize they can never recover this time. Many corporate wanna-bes sacrifice family and friends for that top rung on the ladder, thinking it will solve their problems. They arrive only with more questions and a suitcase full of regrets.

Whether you are chasing money to satisfy your desires or working several jobs to just get by, the sacrifices are seldom worth the results. It's usually an endless race. For centuries, humans have sought the answers to life's deepest question: "How can I be fulfilled and find passion and purpose?" Many seek the answer to this question like the ambitious treasure hunter running in circles. Today the power, position, and prestige the dollar offers is a false god that promises fulfillment and purpose. While money provides the means to accomplish many things, can it really buy happiness?

How much would it take to make you happy? One million dollars, $2 million, or more? Coutts Bank calculated the price of happiness at $4.8 million! That is what it would cost to finance a lifetime of leisure in a five-bedroom house with a maid, a butler, two expensive cars, plus an apartment and yacht in southern France—along with two ritzy vacations a year to get away from the stress of living the high life.

But recent research shows that even this lifestyle does not guarantee happiness. In *Happiness: Lessons from a New Science,* Richard Layard points out that even though income levels have risen over the years, happiness levels have not kept up.[1] Once a person earns enough to meet basic needs, more income has little effect on happiness.

We need money to live and to do almost anything. I'll be the first to tell you I'd rather have more than enough than not enough. Why is it that when you desperately need money, it appears to be the answer to everything but when you have plenty of money you worry about it, spend it on stuff you don't need, and find a way to mess things up?

Solomon, said to be the wisest man who ever lived, told about his experiences of chasing riches. He enjoyed the wealth and pleasures the world offered, but he wanted to see if having more riches would satisfy his inner desires. Ecclesiastes provides us with the chronicle of this adventure and its results—it's all worthless! It's not what it's portrayed to be, not truly satisfying, not healthy, and not worth it. He concluded, "He who loves money will never have enough money to make him happy. It is the same for the one who loves to get many things. This also is for nothing" (Eccles. 5:10, NLV).

The Power of Money

Money is always seeking control of your life. Greed and the desire for more money and the lifestyle it can bring is one of the biggest powers on earth. People forsake family and friends, lie, cheat, steal, and kill for money and its power. Just watch the evening news or read a newspaper and you'll see the result of greed. Recently, executives for bankrupt companies were convicted of corporate crimes. I'm sure many of these executives started out as honest, hardworking people trying to make a good living. But perhaps the lure for more wealth tempted them to give in a little here and there until greed finally caught up with them. It always does.

Greed and corruption are rampant at every level in society—local government, national government, corporate boardrooms, and even in the Church. Can you think of a more powerful force of human nature than the love of money? Perhaps this is why the Bible includes so many references on wealth. Jesus referred to money as a god and said we can either serve mammon (money) or the one true God, but not both (Matt. 6:24).

In his book *Money, Sex, and Power,* Richard J. Foster described money as a "very real spiritual force . . . with a life of its own." He also pointed out that "money is not . . . morally neutral, a resource to be used in good or bad ways depending solely upon our attitude toward it. Mammon is a power that seeks to dominate us . . . hence money is an active agent; it is a law unto itself, it is capable of inspiring devotion."[2]

Money and material possessions bid for your devotion. As a consumer, you are bombarded every day with messages enticing you to indulge in life's pleasures: the latest fashions, luxurious automobiles, gadgets, bigger and better homes, luxury cruises, or overseas vacations. Even children are marketed to as never before. Some authorities estimate that two-thirds of the American economy is driven by consumer spending. Financial traps are set every day, all screaming for our money.

With all the credit card offers, low financing, debt consolidation plans, and scads of other enticements, something continuously demands your money. You must develop a plan for it, or you will never be truly satisfied, even though you gain everything you've always wanted. Money will either destroy your life and purpose or it will help you accomplish it.

Most people have made mistakes with money, such as a

bad investment or a ridiculous purchase. As we make a few mistakes we learn wisdom. However, when money mistakes become habit, we have a problem—money is in the driver's seat and it will take us for a ride.

The ride is fun for a while. You enjoy lots of neat stuff and let everyone know you're in with the culture. But when things start to fall apart, suddenly possessions are not as rewarding as the ads promised. Then you know you've been had. You're under pressure all the time, unable to make ends meet, and wondering how you ended up this way. The price you're paying can't compare to the simple life you once had.

Some Christians believe having worldly wealth is a sin. They think living with little or going without will make them more like Jesus. I can't find Bible teachings that having money is wrong. However, the Bible warns of dangers that wealth can bring to your life. It does say worldly wealth or its pursuit can hinder your devotion to God.

We find a great example of this in Luke 18:24-25. Jesus was speaking to one of the community's young and wealthy religious leaders. After the ruler asked Jesus how to inherit eternal life, Jesus told him the only thing left for him to do was to sell all he had, give to the poor, and follow Him. When the young ruler heard this he was devastated, because he had much wealth. He could not think of departing from this lifestyle, even if he would be wiser.

What was Jesus' response? "How hard it is for rich people to enter God's kingdom! Is it hard for a camel to go through the eye of a needle? It is even harder for the rich to enter God's kingdom!" (NIRV).

How would you respond if God asked you to give everything away? Would you have the faith to do it and trust God to take care of you? That's a tough question. I don't think the message is for you to give away all your money, but Jesus appeared to make this point: when your wealth becomes your life—your god—you are on the wrong track, and it will not lead to paradise.

The apostle Paul also warned Timothy of pitfalls in chasing money: "People who want to be rich fall into all sorts of temptations and traps. They are caught by foolish and harmful desires that drag them down and destroy them" (1 Tim. 6:9, CEV).

Here's the bottom line: If you become too attached to your wealth, or attaining it becomes the overriding factor in your life, you will be dragged down. Your passion and purpose will be destroyed. To prevent money from gripping your life, develop a solid foundation—a purpose and a plan—for your assets. If you don't, when tough times come, your world may fall to pieces.

Harnessing the power of money takes time and commitment. When you put money in its proper place, you can be free from the devotion it seeks. Analyze your life. Ask, "What am I doing with my life? Am I running around trying to achieve status and success?"

Ask God what He wants you to do with your life. What kind of work or life mission do you feel He's created you for? Have you asked God recently how He'd like you to use the time, talents, and money He's given you? You have received a gift—your life and all you will become and possess. You must discern how to use your life so it will glorify your Creator. This is what life is all about.

Do you have a passion? Do you have a dream of what you would like to accomplish? Without discovering your purpose and working toward it, the amount of money you make won't matter. To help illustrate the process of finding your passion and purpose, rank the items below in order of importance. To the side of each, list a description.

____ Family _____

____ God/faith _____

____ Work/career _____

____ Friends _____

____ Hobbies _____

____ Personal interests/dreams _____

____ Other _____

Your priorities should be the reason you work so hard to make money and make your money work for you. By defining the most important things in your life, you can develop a plan for your money to complement and enhance them.

What is consuming your life that doesn't match up with what you know is most important? In order to be fulfilled—no matter your financial condition—you must align your thoughts and plans with your priorities. Write the answers to the above exercise on a piece of paper or a 3 x 5 card where you can regularly see it. This will remind you of the most important things in your life. Are the top three priorities the focus of your life? If not, why not? What are you willing to do to change?

Besides defining the most important things in your life, set goals that will motivate you when times get tough. Your dreams of the person you want to be and the things you'd like to accomplish will give you hope. Proverbs 29:18 says,

"Where there is no vision, the people perish" (KJV). How you view your life is important, but your vision of the future will drive you to do greater things than you could have imagined.

Have you dreamed of what you'd like your future to be? What things would you like to accomplish? Are they realistic but will require supernatural intervention to achieve? I'm not talking about hallucinations of being a rock star or some such fantasy, but something you feel you were created for . . . something only God could put in your heart.

Perhaps this idea or dream repeats itself and is confirmed by events, people, convictions, or experiences. God handcrafted you, and He has something that only you can do. Jeremiah 29:11 says, "'For I know the plans I have for you,' declares the LORD, 'plans to prosper you and not to harm you, plans to give you hope and a future.'"

Everybody needs to dream big dreams. Without a vision of your future, your life will move forward without meaning. These visions and goals should be formulated into a personal mission statement and reviewed, enhanced, defined, and reviewed again. This is an evolving process.

Express to those who are closest to you your idea and vision of who you want to become and what you would like to accomplish. Confide in a friend or mentor who can give you direction, support, and encouragement. As you create a personal mission statement and set life-evolving goals to help you achieve it, your life will have a sense of purpose and fulfillment. To help you define your mission statement, finish these thoughts and dream a little:

If I had all the money in the world, I would like to _____

_____

If I could choose a new career, it would be _____

_____

Why? _____

When my life is over, I want to be remembered as someone who _____

The one thing I want to accomplish before I die is _____

_____

Your answers to these questions will help give meaning to
the race you run. Write these statements and put them where
you can see them every day. These steps are critical to developing an effective plan for accumulating and eventually dis-
tributing your wealth.

What dream or desire of yours is unfulfilled? Is it a longing
that has come to your mind and heart repeatedly? Step toward
your dreams. Seek your desire as if it is a treasure you know is
there. Seek wisdom through mentors and family or friends.
But most of all, ask God for His wisdom and guidance and ask
Him to make your desires known to you.

Some friends of mine, Tom and Karen Randall, are examples of joyously living out their passion. Tom grew up with a
passion for sports. He lettered in four sports and was named a
four-time All-Conference basketball player. He set seven
school records, four conference records, and two national
records. As a college senior, he averaged 31.5 points per game
to lead the nation in scoring.

Tom gave his heart to God while in college, and after he
graduated he followed his heart and joined a team that played
more than 2,000 basketball games internationally. When Tom
was in the Philippines playing basketball, he fell in love with

the people. Filipinos love basketball enough to make it their national sport.

Tom also provided the half-time entertainment with his unicycle and juggling show, which he'd performed on television and in Olympic stadiums, palaces, prisons, universities, military bases, and leper colonies. As Tom became a basketball hero, he told how God changed his life and gave him joy.

Karen's passion is teaching children—she was teaching in the International School. Their hearts went out to the Filipino children, many of whom were abandoned or sold into slavery and prostitution. God began to give Tom and Karen a vision of starting an orphanage. They didn't know how this could happen—they'd need money to buy property and build the facilities to house and educate children.

Tom and Karen asked God to show them what to do. The day Tom shared his vision with Karen, someone offered to give money to start an orphanage in the Philippines. Soon, someone donated property. Now, eight years later, 44 children live in this orphanage. Tom and Karen give the children an education, raise a garden to provide them with rice and vegetables, and have fruit trees. The orphanage also has a gymnasium and a medical clinic.

Because Tom and Karen acted on a God-planted vision of their future, they are helping change lives. By following their passions and acting in faith, not only are they living a purpose-filled, joyful life, but they have also given others the opportunity to serve through their talents and resources. For example, an Australian businessman donated the money to start a piggery for the orphanage, and he taught them how to operate it.

Others have donated prescription drugs and medical equipment that save lives in villages around the orphanage. A young doctor who could have enjoyed a residency in the U.S., but wanted to become a missionary, now operates a hospital that started in Tom and Karen's house. This doctor also trains nurses and other doctors to minister in the villages. Tom and Karen have helped establish two other orphanages in the Philippines where dozens of others also nurture the children.

Tom and Karen live in Oklahoma and travel to the Philippines a couple of months each year to visit their friends and the children. Tom also serves as chaplain for the Senior PGA Tour, providing support and encouragement to players and their families. This couple's story can encourage everyone who seeks true success and joy.

Tom says that if happiness is what you do for yourself, it's like cotton candy—it doesn't last. Circumstances, such as buying a new car or seeing a funny movie, can make us happy some of the time, but eventually that emotion wears off. True joy is found in what you do for others. It comes from the inside; from knowing you are doing what you are supposed to do and having a purpose in helping others. Joy is ongoing. You can experience tough times but still have joy because you know you are part of something bigger than yourself.

Tom says his joy comes from a relationship with Jesus Christ; it's an eternal joy and he feels it most when doing things for others. I believe we are all created for a purpose the almighty God has placed in our hearts even before we were born (see Ps. 139:13; Jer. 1:5). When we see the vision of that purpose and move toward that vision, great things begin to happen. Doors will open and doors will shut. Things will start to fall into place and people will come into our lives to help us accomplish our deepest desires. Money can't produce this. This only comes from within and is God-breathed.

Take some time to discover your vision of what you were born to do. Seek the wisdom of the Scriptures and godly mentors. Don't go to the grave with those desires unfulfilled. Know God wants you to follow your heart's desire. Discovering and living your true passion and purpose will bring you joy no matter your net worth.

Understanding Money

After you have developed your life's purpose and mission statement, the next step is knowing how money can help you accomplish them. So, what is the real value of money? What purpose does money really serve?

Money can take on different roles depending upon its owner, but the basic purpose of money is to sustain you and to provide a lifestyle to meet your goals. It is a means of exchange. You work in exchange for money. You also put money to work to gain more money. Money is important to meet your basic life needs, and it can help make your dreams and desires a reality. Money can put you in a better position to do the things that are important to you and that you value most.

We need money to do just about anything significant. Ecclesiastes 10:19 says, "Laughter and bread go together, and wine gives sparkle to life—but it's money that makes the world go around" (TM).

Christians are also to use money to advance God's kingdom and provide for the needs of His children. How do many view life and money? The American dream: a college degree, a good job, owning a home, having nice cars, lots of toys, retiring in style. These are worthwhile endeavors, but if your life centers around pursuing the American dream, you are constructing your life and financial house on temporary principles—a faulty foundation that is subject to collapse.

Many people try to achieve the American dream but fail to incorporate the financial principles God has so obviously laid out for them. The Bible provides timeless guidelines to help you manage money and to keep you from falling into pitfalls along life's path.

Most money problems stem from childhood perceptions or lack of financial understanding. While you may not have had a parent or mentor to show you money basics—how to budget, save, and invest, and avoid the abuse of borrowing, it's not too late. If you don't know where to start in becoming a better manager of your resources, you may need to look no further than the time-tested principles of Solomon's wisdom.

Many times, Christians are naive in money matters and business dealings—ignoring the present and failing to plan for the future. Instead, they shrug off the blame for their mistakes with "I am not of this world" or "God will provide." Then they don't do their part in using resources and God-given ability to solve problems.

I believe that as children of God, our place here is temporary and we are to fix our minds on things above. I believe God does provide for our needs, but I am also convinced that when things don't go as planned, sometimes because of our bad decisions and actions, we are tempted to say, "It must not have been God's will."

Instead of making excuses, determine to become a good steward of your life and the resources God has blessed you with. Solomon said bad things will happen to good people as well as to those who aren't so good. We shouldn't try to spiritualize every little setback. Sometimes, that's life. It happens to everyone. We should try to learn why it happened, ask God for wisdom, and consider how to avoid such pitfalls in the future.

That's the beauty of seeking wisdom. You can ask direction from somebody who has already been down the road you are starting on. If you had the chance, you wouldn't think twice about asking Warren Buffett a few questions on how to invest your money profitably, would you?

The Bible says a lot about managing money, being resourceful, and seeking wisdom. Scripture indicates that our time on earth is a test of how we manage the resources we have been given. Everything we have is loaned to us. Since we can't take it with us, it's all temporary. People who are good stewards and honor God will be blessed beyond what the human mind can fathom.

In Luke 16:10-12, Jesus pointed out, "He that is faithful with little things is faithful with big things also. He that is not honest with little things is not honest with big things. If you have not been faithful with the riches of this world, who will trust you with true riches? If you have not been faithful in that which belongs to another person, who will give you things to have as your own?" (NLV).

Becoming a faithful steward requires you to become wise about basic money matters and business dealings. You can't get away with sticking your head in the sand, being oblivious to money matters. Here's what Jesus said about worldly wisdom when dealing with money matters, "The master commended the dishonest manager because he had acted shrewdly. For the people of this world are more shrewd in dealing with their own kind than are the people of the light. I tell you, use worldly wealth to gain friends for yourselves, so that when it is gone, you will be welcomed into eternal dwellings" (vv. 8-9).

The key word in this passage is *shrewd*. This word tends to get misused—usually mistaken for someone who is not trustworthy, but it is actually a good trait. A shrewd person is clever and resourceful in practical matters. Being shrewd means calculating the cost of a purchase—both now and in the future. It means making plans for the future and having a plan B just in case plan A doesn't work. Being shrewd is about knowing where the best deals are and not making hasty financial decisions. It also means to learn the options and to be resourceful.

Christians are supposed to be shrewd with their money and business dealings. In the following chapters, we'll discuss how to become shrewd managers of money and life.

In seeking financial help, many go to seminars, buy books and newsletters from financial gurus, or hand over their money to stockbrokers. While some of these may be good, many times they aren't tailored to your specific needs, goals, and desires. If you are going to seek financial advice (and I encourage you to do that, which we'll cover later), you need to go into the relationship with a strong foundation of knowing what you want and what is important to you. If you know your purpose and mission statement in advance, this will help the adviser direct you in making financial decisions. It will also help you weed out advisers who don't understand your needs.

Our society is in information overload. Too much information can stifle your progress, causing indecision and procrastination. Trying to find your own way through the financial information forest can be overwhelming and daunting. You need wisdom—and asking for it is the first step to obtaining it.

The Oracle of Jerusalem: Solomon

When Solomon was young he started a new job as king, taking over the throne from Israel's greatest king, his father, King David. Solomon was inexperienced and overwhelmed. The Bible tells us in 2 Chronicles that God appeared to the young king in a dream and offered to grant anything his heart desired.

What did Solomon ask for? He didn't ask for riches or material possessions—the latest chariot equipped with goblet holders or a built-in surround choir. He asked God for His knowledge and wisdom in guiding His people.

God was pleased with Solomon's request and told Solomon that He would not only give him wisdom but also bless him with riches. We're told that King Solomon had more wealth and wisdom than all other kings. Kings and wise men sought audience with Solomon to hear his God-given wisdom. Second Chronicles says the kings of the earth brought 25 tons of gold yearly to the wise king, which would be approximately $200 million every year! That doesn't include the silver, precious stones, spices, weapons, 12,000 horses, and mules Solomon owned.

What made Solomon so rich wasn't his pursuit of wealth but his desire for wisdom and knowledge. This doesn't mean that if we ask for wisdom, everything will go our way and we will be as rich as Bill Gates or Warren Buffett. In fact, Solomon made a lot of mistakes and did not always please God. But I do believe if you ask for eternal wisdom and apply it in your life, it will help you find peace and fulfillment at any net-worth level.

Solomon's First Lesson

Seek wisdom and understanding more than wealth if you want to achieve true success and joy in life. This is what I call the Solomon factor. We are blessed to have Solomon's teachings recorded in the Bible. These pearls of wisdom have been handed down through many generations and have been continued through Jesus in His life and teachings. It's hard for me to picture Jesus as a money manager, but He spoke more about money than any other subject during His ministry on earth.

Don't you wish you could have dinner with Solomon and gain his knowledge and wisdom firsthand? As long as you have a Bible and this book, you can tap into the timeless principles passed down to us from Solomon. So instead of wearing yourself out chasing riches, come with me on this adventure. Who knows? You might find your life's treasure and success along the way.

Self-Evaluation: Applying the Solomon Factor

When Solomon was crowned king of Israel, he was quite young. He could have asked for anything he wanted, but he asked God for wisdom to know the difference between right and wrong, and wisdom to rule His people. Solomon's prayer was not selfish but was motivated by what was best for others.

If you could ask for anything, what would you choose?

If you received your desire, would it benefit only you?

_____

What are you facing that threatens to overwhelm you?

_____

Ask God right now for the wisdom to help you solve the issue. If you're not sure what to ask for, ask God to show you. Trust Him to grant you the desires of your heart. Trust in His generosity.

Attaining Wisdom

Where does wisdom come from? You won't find it in your horoscope. It comes from God and His Word. "For the LORD gives wisdom, and from his mouth come knowledge and understanding" (Prov. 2:6).

How can you obtain wisdom? Admit your need for wisdom, and implement God's ways in your life. "Showing respect to the LORD will make you wise, and being humble will bring honor to you" (15:33, CEV).

The benefit of wisdom is a rich, blessed life. "Blessed are those who find wisdom, those who gain understanding, for she is more profitable than silver and yields better returns than gold" (3:13-14, TNIV).

If you truly want wisdom for your life, you must take time to seek God's wisdom. Begin by reading at least one chapter a day from Solomon's writing in Proverbs. Find some quiet reflection time to read. Take a pen and paper and write down the concepts that grab your thoughts, and note how you can apply them in your life—how they can help you find direction.

Try this for the next 31 days and see what a difference it makes. Invite God to open your heart and mind and to give you the wisdom He so eagerly wants to give you—and expect results. Make this a life pursuit and reap the rewards of wisdom. "If any of you lacks wisdom, he should ask God, who gives generously to all without finding fault, and it will be given to him. But when he asks, he must believe and not doubt, because he who doubts is like a wave of the sea, blown and tossed by the wind" (James 1:5-6).

Face Your Fears!

What keeps you from stepping out and achieving your dreams? What fears stifle your progress? Fears are mostly self-imposed. They can be rooted from prior experiences and lack of confidence. I remember a high school bully who always poked fun at me. He often tried to pick a fight with me in the presence of a crowd. All year I was frightened and let him push me around.

On the last day of school, something got into me. When I saw him in the hallway, he sneered and challenged me as he had all year long, but this time I said, "Hey, I've had it with you. Meet me across the street right now and let's settle this." I don't know where the courage came from, but I knew I had to face him and move on. So what if I got beat up a little?

I walked across the street without looking back—expecting him to be behind me and thinking about what I would do when we got there. When I arrived on the other side of the street and turned around, he was nowhere. He had chickened out. I won. I overcame my fear—my giant—and was successful. I had to stand up to him. I wasted the whole year worrying about this doofus, and he was nothing.

To overcome your fears you must stand up and face them. Ask, "What's the worst that can happen?" Then move ahead to what you know you should do.

What fears or giants stand between you and your dreams and living out your passion? _____

_____

What's the worst thing that can happen when you face your fear or giant and challenge it? _____

_____

What steps can you take to face and overcome your fears?

_____

_____

2

Put Your Money Where Your Faith Is

A generous man will himself be blessed,
for he shares his food with the poor *(Prov. 22:9)*.

DICK AND JANE arrived back in town from an extended vacation in Florida late at night. The family was asleep in the SUV as Dick pulled into the driveway. As everyone practically sleepwalked to the front door, Dick noticed how dark the house was. At first he thought the front porch lights must have burned out. He suddenly got a heavy feeling in his gut. Dick realized the door was wide open.

"Get back in the car!" Dick whispered to the family, awakening them from their stupor. As Jane and the children ran back to the SUV, they lined the sidewalk and driveway with suitcases and pillows. Dick ran to the car and called 911 on the cell phone. Then he grabbed the flashlight under the driver's seat and proceeded to the front door, while the children cried, "Daddy, don't go, come back!"

Dick scanned the bushes and dark corners with the small flashlight. He reached the front door and stood in the entrance to the living room. He heard nothing and thought, *Maybe we just forgot to shut the door.*

Then he reached for the light switch on the wall . . . click, click . . . nothing. That heavy feeling was back. *Should I run out of here or keep going?* Dick stepped down the hall to the family room and his heart missed a beat. The family room was destroyed. The new, big-screen TV was gone. The 500-watt stereo system and more than 400 compact discs were also gone.

Dick slowly scanned the flashlight to his left to where the new computer system and laser printer had been. Out of the corner of his eye, he saw lights on the front lawn. He dashed for the front door, running right into a policeman. After briefing the police, Dick went to the vehicle where Jane and the kids waited anxiously.

The family stayed in the van until the police finished. They couldn't believe that one of their worst fears had become reality—they had been robbed. Every room in the 4,000-square-foot-house had been ransacked. All valuables had been taken, even Dick's dad's gun collection and his mother's antique china.

As the family huddled together, Jane cried, "How could this happen to us? Why would anybody do this?"

The next week in church, Dick and Jane let the offering plate pass without giving their tithe and offerings. Dick thought, *After all, we've just lost everything in our house. We deserve a break.*

He felt guilty, but with all the bills and Jenny starting college next fall, he figured giving was impossible. *How did we get into this mess?* he wondered. *Better yet, how will we get out of it? Oh, by the way, God, thanks for not letting those thugs get my new bass boat!*

Jane thought, *How will we save enough to replace the stolen property? Insurance will cover only part of it since we didn't have replacement insurance. And we just received the credit card statement for the new digital big screen and the computer system—and that didn't even include the bills from our vacation. How will we pay off the credit cards?*

Dick and Jane are not unusual. They had all the latest high-tech gadgets and toys and an oversized house for their income. Their monthly income was stretched to the max and their giving was based on what they had at the end of the month.

Many good, churchgoing Americans are just like Dick and Jane, working to accumulate lots of possessions while neglecting their financial futures and their relationship with God. In Matt. 6:19-21, Jesus warned us not to have our focus on accumulating a bunch of stuff, "Do not store up for yourselves treasures on earth, where moth and rust destroy, and where thieves break in and steal. But store up for yourselves treasures in heaven, where moth and rust do not destroy, and where thieves do not break in and steal. For where your treasure is, there your heart will be also."

It's OK to enjoy nice possessions, but to keep an eternal perspective, we must realize our things don't last—they break, get stolen, or wear out. As my pastor, Mark Hollingsworth, says, "The greatest things in life are not things." Our lives should not be about pursuing possessions but about building relationships and focusing on the things that God values the most—the souls of His children.

A Debt of Gratitude

When you realize God is the Creator of all you own, including your ability to garner wealth, it helps you live a humble life and feel gratitude. Deuteronomy 8:17-19 says, "Otherwise, you may say in your heart, 'My power and the strength of my hand made me this wealth.' But you shall remember the LORD your God, for it is He who is giving you power to make wealth . . . It shall come about if you ever forget the LORD your God and go after other gods and serve them and worship them, I testify against you today that you will surely perish" (NASB).

If you don't honor God and acknowledge that all income and wealth belong to Him, you're headed down Disappointment Avenue—a dead-end road. If you serve other gods—mammon and possessions—you won't just face financial problems—eventually you'll encounter the ultimate wrath of a holy God. This is a warning from God's Word to not forget where your wealth comes from, and a warning to not live a proud, self-centered life.

You don't have to look far to see examples of this prideful living. As a society, we've become spoiled with expectations of "I deserve it and deserve it *now.*" And we're willing to sacrifice the future for it. While the Bible warns us of serving mammon, we seem to respond better to positive affirmation. Solomon told us a few benefits of honoring the Lord with our income in Prov. 3:7-10: "Do not be wise in your own eyes; fear the LORD and turn away from evil. It will be healing to your body and refreshment to your bones. Honor the LORD from your wealth and from the first of all your produce; so your barns will be filled with plenty and your vats will overflow with new wine" (NASB).

Why do so many of us have trouble following God's principles on handling money? Do we lack dependence on God, thinking we can handle our life better? Or do we have trouble letting go of our money and the security it brings? When we honor God with our wealth, we release mammon's grip on our lives. This is the first step of true financial freedom. This is the foundation on which you must build your financial house.

Honoring the Lord with Your Income and Wealth

One of the ways we honor God and tangibly worship Him is by giving our wealth back to Him. God says in Mal. 3:10, "'Bring the full [tithe] into the storehouse so that there may be food in My house. Test Me in this way,' says the Lord of Hosts. 'See if I will not open the floodgates of heaven and pour out a blessing for you without measure'" (HCSB).

God wants us to give to His work, the Church, to carry out His plans. This message in Malachi tells us that withholding tithe is robbing God. This passage of Scripture tells how God's people were busy making money and building their own houses—living life selfishly—while God's house was neglected. God warned His people through His prophet but also offered a motivating challenge: give the full 10 percent of your income and you will receive more blessings than you can handle.

When we honor God by giving to Him, we find rewards money can't provide: peace, fulfillment, contentment, and purpose. By honoring God with your money, you acknowledge His Lordship in your life and your dependence upon

Him instead of your own strength. When you place your concerns and burdens on Him, He promises to take care of you and your needs.

We should not give just to receive. We should give because we want to honor God and show gratitude. We exist to have fellowship with Him, to worship Him, and to praise Him. When we give just to receive a blessing, we miss the message because we give with selfish motives.

Some Christians don't believe they should give their tithe to their church. They want to give to other ministries or even nonreligious organizations. When creating a financial plan for someone, I review his or her tax returns. The tax returns show not only how much income the person claims but also what that person supports in areas of charitable gifts.

I am continually surprised at how little regular churchgoers give to their churches. Recent studies show that only a small percentage of church members actually tithe. According to an article in the *Omaha World-Herald,* pastors must increasingly confront the issue of money. Most churches rely on pledges, annual appeals, and providing weekly envelopes to raise money. We have yet to see if these techniques, which came into vogue in the early twentieth century, can meet the needs of the twenty-first-century Church.

Americans direct most of their philanthropic dollars to churches, which is good news. But other discouraging trends have emerged. From 1968 to 1997 per-member giving decreased from 3.1 percent of the member's income to 2.6 percent among 29 Protestant denominations. The *Omaha World-Herald* reported that roughly 75 percent of money is given by 25 percent of the people.[1]

Churches face incredible strain as they compete with every other good cause in the community and world. And we encounter some very good causes to give to today. We are deeply moved by the suffering in the world. As believers, we are commanded in the Bible to give to the less fortunate, the poor, and the needy. And we should. People tend to give where they can see it working and helping those who need it most—whether or not that's their church.

Pastors and church leaders could better communicate to their members where the tithe and offerings go—using visuals of the way money touches people in need, pictures of the church involved in the local community and world missions, videos showing testimonies of those who are touched by this giving. Showing these details is more effective than presenting a spreadsheet of the annual budget. The world uses creative means to touch the hearts of potential donors. Pastors and church leaders should take note and better communicate how their church impacts the local community and the world.

When God said, "Bring the whole tithe into the storehouse, that there may be food in my house" (Mal. 3:10), He referred to the local house of God. The Church needs money to carry out the Great Commission. The local church meets so many needs of God's family and the world community: feeding the hungry, providing medical care, building villages and churches, and making new disciples. God wants each of us to be part of a local congregation and to support it with our incomes.

After you have gained control of your finances and have established a surplus, consider giving offerings above the tithe for other charities, needs, and ministries. But first tithe your income to your church. This is the most important step in building a solid foundation for your wealth—understanding that God owns it all. He is just lending it to you.

By giving your 10 percent to the church, you provide for the Lord's work in your community and the world. And you make a commitment to build eternal wealth. By tithing your income, you also loosen mammon's grip, preventing it from choking the life of peace you desire.

Sometimes people ask, "Should I tithe on my gross income (before taxes) or on the net amount (after taxes or "take-home" pay)? As my pastor, Mark Hollingsworth, replies, "Do you want a 'gross' blessing or a 'net' blessing?"

If you aren't in the habit of tithing, starting can be a challenge, especially if finances are tight. If you're questioning whether or not you can give regularly, I have a challenge: Start with something. It may be 5 percent of your income—but do this for six months and commit to increase it to 10 percent within a year.

As you give back to God, ask Him for wisdom to manage your finances. You may need to reduce debt, or you may need to increase income. Trust in Him to provide and resist the temptation to trust in your resources. When you honor God with your finances, you can trust Him to take care of your needs.

I remember many times when my wife, Jana, and I prayed for God to bless our business and take care of our needs. We weren't perfect money managers, but we tithed faithfully even when we couldn't see how we would make it the next month.

One of those times when business was slow we were running out of savings, and we were getting desperate. As Jana and I ate dinner, we discussed paying bills. I felt we should ask God to provide. After all, His Word says to "ask and it will be given to you" (Matt. 7:7). As we prayed, I reminded God of how faithfully we gave our tithe and offerings. We asked God to bless us with new business and provide for our needs. Even our two-year-old son, Gregory, prayed.

The next day I received a call about a client who needed my help. It was more than enough business to meet our needs—and our needs have always been met. That doesn't mean we don't have occasional tough times, but we trust God to provide. God has continued to bless our business, and we have been able to give to other good causes.

Once we create wealth, what do we do with it? "Give," says one successful businesswoman, Mo Anderson. Mo was a farm tenant's daughter in rural Oklahoma. After earning her college degree, she became a music teacher. Years later, she had a successful real estate career. Then the oil bust happened in the late 1980s, plunging her family into a difficult period. She and her husband were in their mid-50s but had to start all over again.

Her strong sense of faith helped guide her. Eventually, she was led to Keller Williams Realty, which she helped transform into Keller Williams International. After joining Keller Williams as CEO in 1995, she grew the company from 35 sales offices to more than 300. She now serves as vice-chair of the board.

Mo credits her family and friends for her success. Her Christian faith serves as her foundation. "My father had an eighth grade education, but he was very wise. He was really an inspiration to me. I would often watch him give away our last dollar to someone who needed it maybe worse than we did. It bothered me, but he'd say, 'The good Lord is just gonna meet our needs and you don't worry,' and sure enough our needs would be met," she said in an interview with *Austin Woman*.

She firmly believes in putting her money where her faith is. Mo started KW Cares, through which Keller Williams associates raise money for those in need. Mo believes that when people gain wealth, they must give to help others. Even during the tough times in her career, she continued to fulfill her financial commitments to Christian organizations. Mo Anderson leads by example and is someone we can learn from.

If you are fortunate to have income to give beyond your tithes, consider where you should place your extra giving. I don't find anything in the Bible that says to give, except to the poor and needy, the widows and the orphans. That pretty much sums it up. It's also pretty broad, leaving much room to help people. We can find many good organizations that help people directly. We can also help people indirectly, such as through medical research and educational institutions.

We encounter many decent causes to give to—animals, the environment—but if you want to plug in to where God's heart is, focus on the areas that help people, especially those who can't help themselves. Thoroughly evaluate any organization to make sure it is financially responsible to an independent entity.

Those who live selfishly and don't share their wealth could be in for some bad times. Just look at Prov. 28:27, "He who gives to the poor will never want, but many bad things will happen to the man who shuts his eyes to the poor" (NLV). King Solomon put it best when he said, "Cast your bread upon the waters, for after many days you will find it again" (Eccles. 11:1). When you help those in need, you will find reward in your efforts, both now and in the future, and you'll find help when you may need it.

Summary Action Plan

1. **Establish tithing on all your income to your church as the foundation of your giving.** Give back to God no matter what your financial condition. Trust God to give you wisdom and blessings for honoring Him.

2. **Review your net worth statement and your budget to maximize giving opportunities.** Ask God for direction and let Him guide you on how and where to spend your income.

3. **Regularly give to the less fortunate.** Giving should be done in secret without strings attached. In your budget, establish a giving program that benefits your church, individuals, or organizations that provide services to the less fortunate.

Self-Evaluation

After reviewing my budget and net worth statement, do I feel I live in reverence and gratitude toward God?

_____

By the way I spend my time and money, do I honor God or am I more interested in seeking wealth and possessions? What needs to change for me to honor God with my time and money? What could I miss by not honoring God with my wealth?

_____

_____

Am I honoring God by giving to His work? Do I consistently give 10 percent of my income to my church? If not, why not? What should I do to align myself according to God's Word? ____

_____

The Tale of Two Givers

Giving—Like a "Rock"

John Davison Rockefeller Sr. (1839—1937) was an American industrialist who was instrumental in the early oil industry. Over the span of 40 years, Rockefeller built Standard Oil into the largest company in the world and was the richest man in the world. He spent his last years focused on philanthropic pursuits, including education and public health.

From his first paycheck, Rockefeller tithed 10 percent of his earnings to his church. As his wealth grew, so did his giving. He eventually gave away about half of his wealth. He supported many church activities and started and funded foundations and trusts that still benefit our society.

An Example of Sacrificial Giving

My maternal grandmother, Julia Gregory (1918-1991), was a divorced, single parent who raised four children on a small farm. While visiting her in the summers, my brother, two sisters, and I had a blast roaming the acreage, playing in the creeks, fishing, building forts, and hunting squirrels.

We also worked in the hay fields and helped with farm chores. With no television in the house, we spent most of our evenings playing games. We also spent a lot of time in the kitchen; Grandma let us help with the cooking and cleanup. Life seemed simple there. The little country church Grandmother attended was a couple of miles west of her home, and we attended every time the doors of the Happy Corner Church of God were open.

My grandmother did whatever the church needed: she taught Sunday School, played the piano, and led the congregational music. She even served as interim pastor for a while. I'll never forget the time she played the old, upright piano during a song with her hand bleeding. While she kept playing, she motioned for me to bring her a tissue so she could keep the blood from running onto the piano.

Grandmother's body was plagued with rheumatoid arthritis. I called her the "bionic grandma" because she had knee replacements on both knees. She eventually had to sell the farm and move into government housing. Even though she lived in constant pain, she had a heart of love and compassion for others. What she could not give in money, she made up with prayers—sometimes spending many hours each day praying for family, friends, her church, and others. She had a heart of giving and selflessness. When Grandma died she had hardly a penny to her name, but her legacy continues today through her family, friends, and the Happy Corner Church community.

Jesus sat near the place where people gave their offerings to the Temple treasury. Many rich people gave large amounts, but a poor widow put in two very small copper coins, worth only a fraction of a penny. Calling to His disciples, Jesus said, "I tell you the truth, this poor widow has put more into the treasury than all the others. They all gave out of their wealth; but she, out of her poverty, put in everything—all she had to live on" (Mark 12:43-44).

3

The Simple Life

{ A pretentious, showy life is an empty life;
a plain and simple life is a full life *(Prov. 13:7, TM)*. }

MIKE AND JAN live in a southwestern metropolitan city. Mike is an electrician's apprentice, and Jan is a stay-at-home mom who home-schools their children, aged six and eight. Mike earns $36,000 per year and has benefits through his employer. They can live comfortably on Mike's salary and put a little money in a savings account and the children's college accounts. Their only debt is the 15-year mortgage on their two-bedroom home, and they are paying extra on it to pay it off in 10 years, which will save them $9,000 in interest charges.

I asked Mike how they survive.

"Well, we don't wear the latest fashions or drive new cars. Occasionally, we would like to have newer things or eat out more. But our used stuff works well and we are healthier because we eat at home," Mike replied.

"It's a challenge to be content in a consumer-driven world. We have to block out the propaganda from advertisements. It's tempting to give in, but if we did, we would be charging stuff on credit cards. That would cost us more, and eventually the stuff would just get old and wear out.

"That's why we buy used stuff. It's much cheaper. Besides, the sacrifices we're making are worth it. Jan can stay at home and have quality time with the kids. I'll be up for a promotion and salary raise next year. We plan on saving some of this money for a bigger house in a couple of years; but we'll keep this house to rent. The raise will also let me contribute to my company's 401(k). We're happy, and I sleep sound at night knowing we have a plan and that God is helping us with our finances."

Mike and Jan are not the usual American family. Many families today struggle just to make ends meet and are burdened with high consumer debt. A lot of people are just one paycheck away from having an automobile or home repossessed. Sadly, many are taking advantage of financing strategies to reposition their debt, creating more cash flow to continue their consumer-driven lifestyle. They are digging a hole so deep that their only way out may be to file bankruptcy.

Living like a Millionaire

When you think of a millionaire, you may think of a lavish lifestyle. Think again. According to *The Millionaire Next Door: The Surprising Secrets of America's Wealthy,* most people don't become millionaires until they are at least 50 years old. Most do not earn high annual incomes but are frugal—and few could have supported a high-consumption lifestyle and become millionaires.[1]

The authors of the book found these common denominators about the wealthy of America: they live below their means; they spend their time, energy, and money efficiently; they place financial independence above social status; their parents did not leave them large inheritances; their adult children are economically self-sufficient; they understand economic opportunities; and they choose occupations with high demand. The biggest factor that profiles the average millionaire today is *frugality*. That's the cornerstone of building wealth.

Based on this data, it appears that Mike and Jan are living like the average millionaire. They're living beneath their income level, they're being resourceful, they focus their money in assets that can appreciate, and they can see opportunity. They have a plan. They are at peace with themselves—not pressured with loads of consumer debt and struggling paycheck to paycheck. Because they can live below their current income level, they'll also be in a position to give more.

What about you? Are you living like a millionaire? Or are you living like the average American—struggling with your finances and with no clear plan for your financial future?

Simplify Your Money

Many people give the impression that they are wealthy when they actually have very little. Big house, high mortgage; expensive cars; high-end clothing; hot vacation spots; living only for today. Several years ago I counseled a couple who had high, six-figure incomes as a doctor and an attorney. They bought everything they wanted, but they also had to borrow money each year to pay their income taxes. Besides their house, which was mortgaged, they had nothing to show for their salaries.

Many people think more money will solve their problems—if they could just win the lottery or get a large inheritance, everything would be better. Some turn to gambling, hoping to hit it big. One man I know has $40.00 deducted from every paycheck to play his state lottery. That's $1,040 per year to play a game with less than a 1 in 1,000,000 chance of winning. Over a 10-year period he would have accumulated $12,000 if he'd put the money into a savings account only making 5 percent compounded monthly. If he got 10 percent on his money through his 401(k) plan, it could grow to over $16,000, not including any employer matching.

While more money can ease some of the pressures, it is only a temporary fix. To get control of your money and be fulfilled, you need a major mind shift on the way you view money and a major change in your habits of handling finances. There is no such thing as a get-rich-quick method if you want wisdom and wealth. Solomon gave this wise bit of advice to those who want to get rich fast, "Good planning and hard work lead to prosperity, but hasty shortcuts lead to poverty" (Prov. 21:5, NLT).

Thinking you will get rich by playing high-risk games and waiting for Ed McMahon to knock at your door will send you to the poor house, but developing a plan for your money and putting it to work will give you better results and make you wealthy and wise. Benjamin Franklin said, "Your net worth to the world is usually determined by what remains after your bad habits are subtracted from your good ones."

Our lives are made up of habits—some good, some bad. Every good action we take, however little it may seem, takes us closer to the person we want to be and to the dreams we hope to achieve.

Our Personal Story

I started my career as an agent for a major insurance company. We had a healthy regular income with benefits and very little overhead. We built up some savings, paid cash for everything, and still had resources left. Then I decided to go on my own. We learned that starting a new business takes time. And while self-employment has rewards, it brings some high price tags. After slow months used up most of our savings, I began to use leverage, better known as borrowing, to keep the business afloat.

As the debt continued to build, we could not pay it off like we'd hoped. Soon we were in a fairly deep hole, so Jana and I started adding up where our money was going. Jana began to cut small living expenses here and there.

One expense to go was cable television—ouch! There went ESPN and my news channels. Jana gave up TV Land. We decided when we paid off some loans and credit cards, our reward would be to turn the cable back on. After cutting expenses in several areas, we were able to reduce our debts in less than two years. And, yes, we turned the cable back on.

The little things you do—done over and over—can lead you down the path of failure and disappointment or down the path of success and accomplishment. To achieve success you must focus on repeatedly doing the small things that bring positive results.

Many habits can hinder a person from achieving financial peace and success. One is overspending your income level. When you spend more than you make, you are deficit spending. It is difficult in our culture to put off the things you want and think you need until you have the cash to pay for them.

Many people give in to the temptation to live above their means. The smaller, day-to-day purchases add up, and before you know it, you're up to your eyeballs in debt.

To overcome the habit of overspending, examine all expenditures and try to harness the desire to spend any amount over a budget-controlled lifestyle. No one likes that word *budget,* but you must put some kind of plan in place to allocate your income. If you don't, it will get misplaced and misspent, and before you know it, you're mesmerized about how you've gotten into this mess! Track everything you spend and subtract this from all of your income sources. The difference is called your cash flow. If you have more expenditure than income, you have a negative cash flow.

Picture yourself in the backyard digging around yourself with a sharp shovel. After each month the hole gets deeper and you're still in the middle, sinking further. This is what happens if you continue to live on a negative cash flow.

If you have money left after all your expenses, then you have a positive cash flow. This puts you in a position of control—but you still have to be a wise money manager.

Your goal should be to adjust your income or expenditures to consistently maintain a positive cash flow. You should use your net cash flow to reduce debt, build savings and investments, and meet specific short- and long-term goals. You can also use the surplus, or extra money, for special giving.

Evaluating your current expenses is the first step to reduce your debts or increase your surplus. To get started you'll need your checkbook ledger and credit card statements. Schedule time to sit down and note where your money is being spent. If you are self-employed and your income varies, use a monthly average based upon an annual amount. Compare your current expenditures to a sample spending guideline budget (provided below). Adjust as necessary to develop a realistic spending plan that honors God and allows for savings and debt reduction.

Spending Guidelines

Here is a sample spending plan to use as a guideline (based upon a family of four, take-home pay of $60,000).

Housing	27 percent
Transportation	15 percent
Food	12 percent
Tithing	10 percent
Savings	10 percent
Medical	6 percent
Clothing	5 percent
Personal Insurance	5 percent
Miscellaneous*	10 percent

*(Entertainment, gifts, household items, etc.)

No set amount works for everyone. Your budget should be tailored to your spending needs. For example, housing in your area may be higher or lower than the national average. Or if you are self-employed, your insurance and medical costs may exceed those of someone who has company benefits. Also, if you have consumer debt, you should apply money toward paying that and may not be able to allocate as much to savings or other items, until the debt is paid off.

If you have family members, seek their cooperation—this will be important for a spending plan to succeed. Have a meeting to set out goals and share why you are adjusting spending habits.

Talk to your children about the value of money and the negative effects of consumer debt. Make this a positive experience each member can relate to. For example, if you set out a plan to reduce spending in one area and apply it toward paying off a loan, when the loan is paid, reward each person. It could be something small, like a fun toy or new pair of shoes they've wanted, or a trip to the amusement park. The important thing is to set goals, let the family participate, and reward everyone when the goals are met. Celebrate in your success.

If you do this, everyone will be more willing to participate; it can be something you'll look forward to. You will also move closer to your financial goals.

Here are a few basic guidelines to consider when drafting your spending plan:

1. **Tithe: Pay God First.** Put 10 percent of each paycheck in a tithe envelope or allocate it in your checking account. Write the tithe check as soon as you make your deposit—this way you won't forget. Something else will always come along and try to take its place.

Take your tithe to church with you and place it in the offering plate. Giving is part of your worship experience. Letting children help give the tithe encourages them to build a healthy relationship with God and money. Paying your tithe should have top priority.

2. **Savings: Pay Yourself Second.** Allocate some savings from each paycheck. Save at least two weeks of your pay as soon as possible in a savings account or money market. This will be your emergency fund for unexpected expenses. As your income increases and your debts reduce, save 15 percent to 20 percent of your income. Some of this will be for long-

term goals, like college and retirement; and some for shorter-term goals, like a new car purchase or family vacation.

If you don't have enough money to pay your bills each month, continue to cut back on unnecessary items. If you can't save after cutting expenses, then consider getting a part-time job until you have built up your savings to at least one month of income needs.

3. Debt: Lighten Your Load. If you have consumer debt, pay it off and free yourself as soon as possible. Debt is a roadblock to financial security. It is your master; it obligates your future.

The concepts of reducing debt are simple—change spending habits. But sticking to your debt reduction plan takes effort. The sooner you start, the better off you'll be. I'll tell you about a rapid debt reduction plan in the next chapter.

4. Retirement: Contribute to a Company Retirement Plan or IRA. Start contributing to a company-sponsored retirement plan. If you work for a company that makes a matching contribution, contribute the percentage of your salary that is matched dollar-for-dollar. For example: if your employer will match your contribution up to the first 5 percent, start contributing to your plan at that level. By doing so, you make 100 percent return on your money.

As your income increases and your debts are reduced, save up to 15 percent of your income. You may be able to contribute to a traditional Individual Retirement Account (IRA) or a Roth IRA as well as to your company-sponsored plan. Contributions to your company plan are tax deductible; contributions to a traditional IRA may also be deductible, depending on your income level. These tax deductions can save you hundreds of tax dollars every year.

5. Taxes: Pay Your Fair Share, but No More. Nothing is illegal about finding ways to reduce your taxes. Jesus told His disciples in Matt. 22:21, "Give to Caesar what is Caesar's, and to God what is God's." We should pay our taxes as good citizens of our society, but you can legally reduce the amount of taxes you pay.

If you are receiving more than $500 per year in refunds, you are probably not claiming enough exemptions. Consider increasing your exemptions to reduce the taxes withheld from your paycheck. Apply this extra income to your debt-reduction plan or to savings. Adding it to a 401(k) or other tax-deductible plan will also reduce your taxes.

If you're self-employed, set aside at least 25 percent of every paycheck to use for quarterly tax payments. Be sure to fund these tax amounts every paycheck so you won't get behind; and don't use these funds except for taxes.

6. Insurance: Prepare for the Unexpected. Make sure you have adequate insurance. Designate a portion of your budget to protect you and your assets: your health-care needs, your automobiles, your home and property, your income, and your life.

Many resources are available to help you budget. If you like to use your computer to organize your spending, use QuickBooks or other software. You can categorize each expense and the program will help you determine if you have tax-sensitive items. If you keep this current each month, it will help you at tax time.

If you don't want to use a computer, try the envelope system. Create one envelope for each spending category. When you receive your money, put the amount you've budgeted into each envelope and use the money in that envelope only for that item. This helps you keep track of all your income and your bills, and accounts for savings and goals.

A good resource for the envelope system is at www.envelope budgeting.com. For an electronic version of the envelope system, the Personal Mvelopes system is a great tool: www.mvelopes.com or 866-367-4262.

Check out several references and use a system that is compatible with your needs. Start tracking all of your expenses and finding ways to reallocate them in areas to help you reach your goals.

If you are going to overspend in any area, it should be on assets that appreciate in value, such as your home. I'm sure you've seen people driving fancy cars but living in a mobile home or renting an apartment. That picture doesn't make sense. Focusing your dollars on depreciating assets is bad stewardship.

Review your current spending habits and begin adjusting them—putting your money in assets that appreciate or in reducing consumer debts. If you don't have enough cash flow each month to save and invest, you may need to take some drastic measures. For example, if you have a couple of car loans, you may need to sell one or both cars, pay off the loans, and purchase more affordable vehicles.

Then start building your savings, paying debt, and investing in appreciating assets. You can look in many other areas when trying to find extra funds. Here are a few ideas:

- Transfer high-interest cards to low-interest ones. Look for a zero interest rate card. Many card companies will offer them up to a full year without interest charges, as a teaser to get you to move your money; but make sure you pay extra on the amount to pay off early. After the initial zero percent, the rate can move to rates of 20 percent or more—so read the fine print.

- Take your lunch to work. Eat out less. By brown-bagging it just two days a week, saving $6.00 each time in a savings plan growing at 7 percent, you'll accumulate $9,225 dollars in 10 years.

- Eat at home before going to ball games, amusement parks, fairs, or even the grocery store.

- Cancel cable TV or premium channels. You can turn it back on as a reward for reducing debt. Watching television is one of the biggest time wasters in America.

- Review auto/home insurance and consider raising deductibles. Full coverage (collision and comprehensive) is the most expensive part of your auto insurance. Review your coverage and raise your deductibles if they are lower than $500. For used cars that are four years old or more, go with a $1,000 deductible. Consider carrying only liability coverage on older, paid-for vehicles.

- Use coupons (entertainment books, coupons online, etc.). We take the Sunday paper just for the coupons and my wife saves $50.00 each month on things we need. Get in the habit of cutting coupons. Set up a filing system for your coupons and take it when you shop.

- Trade services with friends or family (babysitting, haircuts, yard work, ironing, etc.). We all are good at something. If someone needs your services, ask him or her to trade for something you could use.

- Refinance home mortgage to lower interest rates. You need to reduce your rate by two percentage points to make it worth the cost.
- Sell a car that you owe on, and buy a used one that gets good gas mileage. With higher gas prices, a fuel-efficient vehicle can save you hundreds of dollars each year.
- Have a garage sale. Your junk may be someone else's treasure.
- Never pay retail—negotiate! Wait for what you need to go on sale or buy a used item. When negotiating, start with a ridiculously low amount and work your way up.

Review your spending habits and look for ways to find extra money to apply to debt reduction, savings, and giving. Continue this even after you have reduced your debts. This will put you in a better position to fulfill your life purpose.

If you can't make ends meet or need to reduce debts, here are a few more tips to help you free up cash flow:

1. **Starbucks or 10 Bucks?** I love a good cup of coffee at Starbucks, but I don't buy it at Starbucks every day. I buy a big bag of beans and make it at the office or home. If you have a latte five days a week at $3.75 a pop, after 25 years you could have had enough money to buy a small house, at $76,981 ($975/year @ 8%). Remember, small amounts over time add up to bigger amounts. Don't give up coffee or lattes —just find a more affordable way to have what you like.

2. **Buy Value Generic or Off-brand Items.**
   - Prescription drugs and over-the-counter medications
   - Clothes and shoes

- Household items: cleaners, soaps, paper products
- Vitamins and minerals
- Sporting goods

3. **Buy Previously Owned Items.**
   - Automobiles
   - Furniture—especially if you have young kids!
   - Audio/video gadgets
   - Yard tools/machinery

Millionaires, and billionaires like Warren Buffett, invest in companies that have intrinsic value. They look for companies that are priced low but have high potential earnings. It takes time to identify these opportunities, but once they're found, they can reap many rewards.

The same concept applies toward how you spend money. No matter how much money you accumulate, spend it in areas that have value. Value doesn't always mean the cheapest but includes what you get for your money. Is it a good product or service relative to the marketplace of similar items?

Application: Get Organized in Three Steps

1. **Prepare a Cash Flow Report.** List your income sources and expenses. You'll need a cash flow work sheet, your checkbook ledger or credit card statement, your pay stub(s), and a calculator.

The Goal:

- Get a clear, honest picture of where your income is going. Compare your expenses to a sample spending guideline.
- Create a surplus by eliminating any unnecessary spending and reallocate those funds to priority items. Use the surplus to build savings and reduce debts.

2. Create a Debt/Creditor Inventory. List outstanding debts—including credit cards, car loans, and other debt. Include the balance owed, term of loan, and monthly payment. The Goal:

- Get a current picture of what you owe. You'll want to free yourself from these creditors. (More on this later.)

3. Complete a Balance Sheet or Net Worth Statement. Use an asset and liabilities worksheet listing your assets: your home, vehicles, miscellaneous property, retirement accounts, personal investments, savings, and so forth. Then list what you owe on each asset. This will help you determine your net worth (assets minus your liabilities) and determine your tendency to borrow. The Goal:

- Your net worth statement is the condition of your financial health. This will also be used to project the growth of your estate for retirement income needs and future goals. You should update your net worth statement at least twice a year. Your goal is to increase your net worth over time and free yourself of liabilities.

Budgeting Your Time

It is hard to not talk about time when you deal with money and goals. Have you ever noticed that when you have more time on your hands you feel more relaxed, can breathe more easily, and can think more clearly? How you manage your time could have the biggest impact on your life—more than anything else you do.

In our fast-paced society, time is money. Money may not buy you happiness, and it definitely can't buy you time. Time is the only thing we were born with; it's free, given to everyone. We don't know how much of it we have overall, but we all have the same amount of time each day—whether rich or poor, young or old. Managing your time should be a priority if you are serious about reaching your goals and achieving your life purpose.

We can't always control time issues, such as a traffic jam, waiting in a checkout line, waiting to see your doctor, being interrupted by unexpected phone calls or drop-ins; or having to arrive at the airport two hours before the flight. During these times we all learn patience. Integrating even small things throughout the day can chip away at wasted time and make a big difference. When you know time delays might happen, plan to be productive—have a book to read, paperwork to complete, return phone calls, listen to a book on tape, or write notes. Get in the habit of planning ahead to use your time more effectively during uncontrolled downtime. You'll be less stressed and accomplish more.

Here are a few more tips to make your time more effective:

- Keep a daily journal of the time you spend every hour. Stop at the end of each hour, if possible, and write down everything that happened. Note phone calls, meetings, and other items that may require follow-up. Try this for 30 days and you'll become more aware of your time and more organized. After the first week, review each day and adjust your activities to reduce time wasters so you can better reach your weekly and life goals.

- Remove clutter in your work area. Clutter causes confusion, makes it harder to find things, and subconsciously tells you that you are disorganized.

- Plan the next day each night. Make a to-do list and prioritize tasks. Planning the day before lets your mind process what you need to accomplish. Schedule specific tasks using a daily or weekly calendar.

- Schedule times to return phone calls and e-mails. Have messages taken or placed in voice mail. Let your callers know when they can expect to hear back from you. Check and return e-mail once in the morning and once before the day is done. This will limit interruptions and let you focus on tasks at hand.

- Keep your office door closed to reduce interruptions when working on detailed or time-sensitive projects.

- Hold brief organizational meetings before a project starts, plan extra time for contingencies, and set timeline goals for each person.

- Start planning events and projects six months to one year in advance. Prepare calendar and agenda for projects, assign tasks with deadlines. Meet frequently to review progress and adjust goals as needed.

- Delegate tasks that assistants, coworkers, or family members can perform. Training them may take time initially but could save hours in the days ahead.

- Schedule personal or family time in advance and stick to it like any other appointment.

- Read a book or take a course in organization and time management or hire a personal coach in this area.

- Reduce time-robbing activities, such as casual Web-surfing and watching excessive television.

Where's the Remote?

Watching too much television is probably the biggest time waster. According to the A.C. Nielsen Co., the average American watches 4 hours of TV each day (or 28 hours per week, or two months per year). In a 75-year life, that person will have spent 13 years glued to the tube. Americans watch 250 billion hours of TV per month.

What would happen if a person cut back his or her television time to one hour a day? He or she would have three additional hours to accomplish more meaningful tasks—even going to bed earlier for needed rest. We all need a break occasionally, but the next time you catch yourself watching television, ask if this is the best use of your time. If you are watching several hours of television a day, find more rewarding, creative, and relationship-building activities to fill that void. Then, reward yourself with your favorite show after you have accomplished a goal for the day.

For television watchers, one of the best time-saving inventions is the digital video recorder (DVR). The DVR lets you tape all of your favorite shows to view while fast-forwarding through the commercials. Most one-hour shows have about 20 minutes of commercials. Invest in a DVR and cut your TV viewing time by 30 percent!

Sleep on It

In Prov. 20:13, Solomon said, "Do not love sleep or you will grow poor; stay awake and you will have food to spare." Waking up early and getting a head start can add more quality time in your work schedule and can help you be more productive. Rising early brings many rewards. If you rose an hour earlier each day, you would add 25 hours per month or 300 hours per year—that's 3,000 hours every 10 years—to your waking schedule.

What is your time worth? If you make $50,000 per year, that equals $24.00 per hour (based on a 40-hour workweek). If your time is worth $24.00 per hour, rising one hour earlier is equivalent to $7,200 per year, over 10 years it amounts to $72,000.

If you can't go to work earlier, use this time to work on ideas and goal-setting or take a class to learn a new trade to increase your income potential. By getting an early start, you are usually up before the rest of the world—when it's quieter. Use this time to start the day with prayer and meditation, to plan the day, or to get a good workout.

Planning your day in advance helps you prioritize what you need to accomplish. It also will help you be better prepared to solve problems or deal with tough issues. If you want to accomplish your dreams and goals, manage your time effectively. Rising early and getting a head start on your day is one of the most important habits you can develop.

Don't get me wrong; sleep is very important. It helps the body rejuvenate. How much sleep should you get? Everyone is different. Experts say children and teenagers need as much as 10 hours a night. The average adult functions best with seven to eight hours of sleep.

I went five years averaging less than five hours of restless sleep per night. It affected my attitude, productivity, and performance. I was finally diagnosed with sleep apnea and got a continuous airflow machine that helps me sleep. As a result, I feel less stressed and less fatigued during the day and can accomplish more.

Sleep is important, but too much of it is not good stewardship. If you have trouble sleeping, seek professional help. This could add hours to your year, years to your life, and life to your day. Solomon warned those who are lazy and love sleep, "How long before you get out of bed? A nap here, a nap there, a day off here, a day off there, sit back, take it easy—do you know what comes next? Just this: You can look forward to a dirt-poor life, poverty your permanent houseguest" (Prov. 6:10-11, TM).

To be successful with your money you must be able to first manage the simple things in life—basic needs like time and sleep. How you live will be reflected in your dollars and cents.

What steps do you need to take to simplify your life and spend your time more wisely? Are you spending your time on things that will give your priorities in life maximum benefit?

Consider my friend Quin Tran's story. She was the first Asian-American woman to anchor a prime-time newscast in Oklahoma City. Quin was always on the go; she never refused a story. After she was in the business for a dozen years, her biggest blessing arrived—her baby daughter. Priorities quickly changed. She struggled with the guilt of working long days and having few hours with her child. When the baby turned two, Quin made a career change that meant a pay cut. The trade-off was that it would simplify her life and give her more time with her daughter.

In Quin's new job she served as the public information officer for a major health care organization that offered on-site childcare, solving one of her problems.

While the work hours were more predictable, there were other strings attached. Instead of one pager, she had two. Instead of one television station, there were five—plus radio stations, newspapers, and other media inquiries to respond to.

Quin's life wasn't really simpler, but this career change was in the best interest of her family. She made her decision based on her priority.

4

Drowning in Debt

{
The poor are always ruled over by the rich,
so don't borrow and put yourself
under their power *(Prov. 22:7, TM)*.
}

FOR GENERATIONS, people have been drowning in debt. History tells us that before the nineteenth century, people were imprisoned for failing to pay their debts. Debtors remained there until their debts were paid, which also included expenses for the prison stay and food.

While our society no longer incarcerates and enslaves debtors, there are penalties for not paying your debt on time. Failing to pay the minimum due will cost you even more— and that is how people drown in debt today.

According to a study by DEMOS, between 1989 and 2001 credit card debt in America almost tripled, from $238 billion to $692 billion. During this time, the savings rate steadily declined, and the number of people filing for bankruptcy jumped 125 percent. The report also reveals that many Americans have borrowed so much not necessarily because of frivolous consumption but from stagnant or declining wages, job displacement, and rising health-care costs.

A more recent study finds that in the race to get ahead economically, America's young workers are falling behind. Between 2001 and 2004, income fell 8 percent, adjusted for inflation, for those under 35; and 9 percent for those aged 35 to 44. The numbers add new weight to longstanding concerns about whether younger generations of Americans will achieve living standards equal to or better than those of their parents.

The rising cost of higher education and health care and changing patterns of family life are among the factors that make the career environment tougher, economists say. The past few decades have seen a rise of single-parent and non-family households, which typically have lower incomes than married-couple households. Higher debt loads will hinder many Americans from getting ahead.

Over the past decade, the volume of federal student loans tripled, reaching $85 billion in new loans last year, according to *Generation Debt* by Anya Kamenetz.[1] Nearly a quarter of college students use credit cards to pay some of their tuition costs.

Is It Wrong to Borrow?

The Bible doesn't say it's wrong to borrow. Examine your motives for borrowing and look at what the Bible says (Prov. 28:22; Matt. 6:24; Luke 8:14).

Borrowing money is common in our economy. Most people would not be able to afford a home if they couldn't borrow money to pay for it. Businesses and corporations regularly borrow money to cover overhead and expansion needs. Some companies even borrow money to pay the interest on their loans or to pay their bond holders. The U.S. government borrows money from those who buy their treasuries, and, yes, the government continues to borrow money to pay interest to its lenders.

Nothing is wrong with borrowing as long as the person or entity can pay off the note within a reasonable time frame. Borrowing is nothing more than using leverage. Leverage is the use of various financial instruments or borrowed capital to increase the potential return of an investment; the amount of debt used to finance a firm's assets.

In simple terms, leverage means that if I wanted to invest or expand my business so I could earn 20 percent on every dollar invested, I could borrow the money on a short-term basis, say, at a 7 percent annual rate. This would keep my liquid cash available for operations or other company needs. When the additional income comes in from the expansion, I start paying off the loan. I use leverage to enhance my ability to make money.

People who are overloaded with debt are usually living above their means. They spend more than they earn, racking up thousands of dollars on credit cards. Many people who live above their means borrow more money than they can repay in a short period. Time will only compound the problem. Take a look at this example of not paying off your debts quickly:

Credit card balance	$9,000
Interest rate	15%
Minimum payment	3% of monthly balance
Time to pay off	231 months or 19.25 years
Total interest paid	$6,290.87!

In this example of paying the minimum balance, it would

take more than 19 years to repay the loan balance, resulting in more than $6,290 in interest charges. Compare this to the example below, which shows the benefits of paying debts sooner:

Credit card balance	$9,000
Interest rate	15%
Payment	$600 monthly
Time to pay off	17 months or 1.5 years
Total interest paid	$1,029.61

In this example, if you increased your minimum payment by an extra few hundred dollars to $600 per month, you would pay the loan balance in one year and five months and save $5,261 in interest! This is amazing!

If you have outstanding loans, always pay extra on them to pay them off early. If you don't, it will cost you dearly.

Do you have a tough time paying all your bills and barely have enough money at the end of the month? Chances are that you have a high debt-to-income ratio. The debt-to-income ratio (DTI) is a personal-finance measure comparing a person's debt payments to his or her income.

This measure is important in the lending industry as it helps lenders know how likely they are to receive payments from the borrower. To find out your DTI ratio, review your cash flow worksheet and debt/creditor work sheet. Add your debt payments and divide this number into your net income (after taxes). If your DTI ratio is more than 35 percent, then you are highly leveraged and should put your debt-reduction plan in high gear—and don't borrow anything else. Even after you've paid your current debts, keep your borrowing to a minimum.

Three Wise Rules for Buying on Credit

1. Rule No. 1. Never buy anything on credit that doesn't *appreciate* in value. Will the value of the item lessen over time?

2. Rule No. 2. The payments must not be so high that they strain your budget and jeopardize other important financial goals (i.e., retirement, college savings).

3. Rule No. 3. Never pay the full term of the loan, even your home mortgage. Make extra payments and pay off early—saving thousands of dollars in interest.

Also, be careful about cosigning for others. As a cosigner you are obligated to pay the loan if the other person cannot pay. If the person needs a cosigner on a loan, there's a good chance that person may not be able to follow through on the commitment.

Most people who cosign are parents helping their children. If your child needs a cosigner, make sure the loan is collateralized and you have the right to the property if the child can't pay.

Recently a client showed me letters from creditors who filed "failure to pay" notices because the client's daughter defaulted several service contracts the parents had cosigned 15 years previously. They now expect the parents to pay the obligation. The parents had no idea the agreement was still enforceable.

Don't obligate yourself when you have no control. Avoid cosigning, especially on credit cards and cell phones. As Solomon said, "My child, suppose you agree to pay the debt of someone who cannot repay a loan. Then you are trapped by your own words, and you are now in the power of someone else. Here is what you should do: Go and beg for permission to call off the agreement. Do this before you fall asleep or even get sleepy. Save yourself, just as a deer or bird tries to escape from a hunter" (Prov. 6:1-5, CEV).

Reducing Your Debts in Three Simple Steps

1. **Step No. 1: Take Inventory.** You need to know who you owe money and how much. Gather your credit card, auto loans, mortgage, and other statements. Use your debt/creditor work sheet at the end of this chapter to write down all of your loans and the amount you are paying on each balance. Then complete your cash-flow (budget) report listing all of your income and expenses. You may need to use your checkbook ledger as a reference. Complete this step first to get a complete picture of your situation.

2. **Step No. 2: Assess Your Situation.** This is the examination phase. Look for expenditures that you can eliminate. Are funds going to things you really don't need? If so, eliminate them. Find extra funds to reduce your debts and maximize savings.

Your first priority should be to store enough savings in a safe, liquid account that will be used only for emergencies. This fund should equal at least one month of living expenses. You don't have to save a full month of income before you start paying your debts. You can do both at once. For example: let's assume you found an extra $200 per month you could apply to your debts. If you don't have an emergency fund, apply $100 per month to a savings account and the other $100 to your debt elimination plan. When you've saved enough to cover one month of income needs, focus the whole $200 to reducing debts.

3. **Step No. 3: Attack and Eliminate!** After step 2, the goal will be to reduce your credit card debt and other consumer loans (i.e., car loans, department stores) first. Since these loans are typically the most expensive and the assets depreciate in value, pay these off quickly.

Rank your loan balances from the smallest to the largest, including your home mortgage. Apply the extra money you found in step 2 to your smallest loan balance payment until it is eliminated. Then take the total payments you were paying on the first loan and attack the second loan.

Keep paying your normal payments on all of your loan balances. Continue attacking until all of your loans are eliminated. Try not to charge additional items during your debt elimination program.

After you've paid your consumer loans, use some of your extra monthly income to pay extra on your home mortgage. Continue to build your savings and contribute to a tax-deductible retirement plan, and if you're eligible, start a Roth IRA.

This method is referred to as the snowball method because you start with a small amount and as you pay off each balance the amount applied to the next one gets bigger—compounding the effect.

Before you know it, you'll make more and more progress in eliminating debt until you are free from it. List your loans and mortgages to help you prioritize your debt reduction plan.

Example of the snowball debt-reduction plan:

List all current loans with the smallest balance first and then the next highest amount, and so on.

Account/Rate	Balance	Monthly Payment	Normal Paid Off	Total Charges
Credit Card A 15%	$600	$25	29 months	$117.83
Credit Card B 15%	$2,500	$75	44 months	$754.26
Credit Card C 12%	$3,500	$105	41 months	$778.73
Car Loan 6%	$6,000	$150	37 months	$580.08
Totals	$12,600	$355		$2,230.90

Start finding additional funds in your budget by reducing unnecessary spending or by increasing your income. Apply additional amounts to Credit Card A. Let's say you find $100 per month to apply toward Credit Card A, making your total payment of $125 per month—allowing you to pay off the loan in 5 months, instead of the 29 months at the current $25 per month payment. After the fifth month, take the $125 payment you were making on Credit Card A and apply it to Credit Card B, increasing the payment to $200. You'll pay this loan off in 18 months versus 44 months.

Continue this total payment of $200 to Credit Card C in 19 months, increasing the total monthly amount to $305. Credit Card C would then be paid in 25 months versus 41 months.

Now for the last loan, take the $305 and apply it to the auto loan in the 25th month—making for a total payment of $455. You will pay off the auto loan in 32 months versus 35 months. Under this scenario, you would be debt free in just 32 months versus 44 months.

The key is to not spend the extra money from the paid off debt but to move it forward to the next one. Like any system, it takes discipline to stick to your plan until you are debt free.

Be careful to not get caught up in the debt consolidation trap. Hundreds of mortgage companies are dying for you to let them loan you a big chunk of money to wrap up all your credit card debts, loans, and home mortgage into one easy plan and lower your payments.

I seldom encourage people to consolidate their debts. Even though it can free additional cash flow due to lower payments, it can actually cost you more.

For example, most debt consolidation plans are built around taking the equity from your home and doing a new mortgage that includes your credit card and other loans into a new 30-year mortgage. By stretching out the term to 30 years, the monthly payment is less than the total of all your credit cards and other loans.

Here's the problem: even though the annual percentage rate on the 30-year mortgage is lower; you still end up paying more because of the longer time. The only way for this debt consolidation plan to work is to commit the extra monthly savings back into the new mortgage and apply the rest toward a savings account to cover emergencies.

Many people who can't control their spending will take that extra money each month and blow it on stuff or rack up new credit card debt. It's a false sense of security and a temporary fix. Look for yourself in this example:

Current Loans to Be Consolidated

Amount Owed	Monthly Payment	Interest Rate
Credit cards ($9,000.00)	$360.00	15.00 percent
Installment loans ($20,056.05)	$875.00	6.56 percent
Existing mortgage loans ($118,618.11)	$900.00	7.80 percent
Totals ($147,674.17)	$2,135.00	8.07 percent

New Consolidated Mortgage Loan

Mortgage amount	$147,674.00
Monthly payment	$933.40
Interest rate	6.50 percent
Term	30 years

Total interest	$188,349.95
($31,095.27 more than your current debt situation)	
First year tax savings*	$2,854.17
(with a combined state and federal income tax rate of 25.00 percent)	

As you can see, over a period of years, the debt consolidation plan costs an additional $31,095.27, compared to paying full-term on the higher interest rate loans.

Keep Score

Too much debt will negatively affect your credit score. What can a bad score cost you?

Credit Score	Percentage
499 and below	1 percent
500-549	5 percent
550-599	7 percent
600-649	11 percent
650-699	16 percent
700-749	20 percent
749-799	29 percent
800 and above	11 percent

The better your score, the lower your interest; this can save you money. The difference between a score of 530 and a score of 730 is approximately 3.5 percentage points. On a $100,000 30-year mortgage, that difference would add up to $85,000 in additional interest charges; this amount equals an additional monthly payment of over $200 per month.

Can you afford to throw away $85,000 in extra charges over the next 30 years? If you don't get a handle on your debt, you very easily could.

According to Bankrate.com, these key factors determine your credit score:

1. How you pay your bills (35 percent of score). Paying your bills on time is the key. Collection agency involvement and declaring bankruptcy are negatives.

2. The amount you owe and the amount you have available (30 percent of score). The more credit you have access to, the lower this score.

3. Length of credit history (15 percent of score). The longer the good history, the better.

4. Your mix of credit (10 percent of score). Different types of credit history (i.e., credit card, mortgages, installment loans).

5. New credit applications (10 percent of score). The more credit applications you're filling out, the lower this score.

Keeping your credit score strong will put you in a better position to borrow money and get a better deal. It may also affect your chances of getting a job since most employers run a credit check on prospective employees. Your credit score can say a lot about your work ethic and character.

You can determine your score unofficially with a free estimator at Bankrate.com. Other companies provide you with a credit report and score for a fee. Here is a list of reputable companies you can contact:

Equifax: www.equifax.com or 800-685-1111

Experian: www.experian.com or 800-397-3742

TransUnion: www.transunion.com or 877-322-8228

Reduce Spending

Two major areas to reduce spending and build wealth faster:

1. Eating Out. Eating out can be expensive. A family of four eating out four times a week could easily spend $100 a week. That's $5,200 every year—$52,000 over 10 years!

You have to eat; and with busy schedules it's convenient to hit a drive-through. If you are a single parent, or both spouses work, planning meals at home takes extra time, but the effort may be worth it. Meals at home can be healthier for you, cost much less, and create more quality time with your family. Make eating at home a priority and watch your family relationships and bank account grow.

2. Your Car. Is your car driving you to the poor house? Transportation can be the second largest part of your budget, next to your home mortgage. Some people pay $50,000 or more on transportation over six years. Unless you've paid off all consumer debts, have saved for your children's college, and are saving at least 10 percent for your nest egg, you should drive the most affordable car you can.

I buy preowned, low mileage, good, clean vehicles. New cars are nice, but they are expensive and depreciate quickly. Let's say you need a vehicle and want something that looks nice, is dependable, and gets decent gas mileage. Instead of buying a brand-new Lexus, look at one that's a year or two old. You've just saved yourself $20,000! Go one further: if you downgrade to an Avalon, just below the Lexus, you can save $30,000 depending on the vehicle's age.

Used cars are almost as good as new and will cost you less in insurance. I will sometimes purchase an extended warranty if the manufacturer's warranty is expired. It paid off nicely one time when the transmission went out on a vehicle.

Go online to compare prices. Look for ways to save on

your transportation and put the savings toward assets that appreciate, such as your home. Think about it: your vehicle depreciates in value every year. After 20 years of putting thousands of dollars into your vehicles, what do you get? What if you were to save at least $15,000 every 5 years from buying a preowned vehicle? That would be $60,000 saved over 24 years, not including finance charges. You can use the savings toward reaching your goals.

Your Home

Save $95,000 on Your Home!

Your home is your haven. At the end of the day, when you're tired, you want to go home. You'll probably spend most of your money on your home. The U.S. average purchase price for a single-family home reached $264,540 in October 2004, according to the Federal Housing Finance Board.

Below is an example of a 30-year mortgage at 6 percent on a principal loan balance of $150,000. If you were to pay the full term of this loan, you will have paid more than $173,758 in interest, bringing the home cost to $323,758. Compare this to the 15-year mortgage, and the total interest would be only $77,842, a $95,916 difference in interest rate charges. Even though you may not own the same house for 30 years, you can apply this concept for every 30-year mortgage on each home you buy.

Be careful of creative financing strategies that many mortgage companies offer. Buying too much house and trying to finance it on an interest-only loan could be hazardous, especially if you are delinquent or if interest rates rise. You'll be stuck with a higher interest rate and payment.

According to the Mortgage Bankers Association, mortgage delinquencies are increasing due to rising interest rates and other economic factors, especially for those with adjustable-rate and subprime mortgages. When financing your home, lock in rates when they're lower and pay a shorter term.

If you're already purchasing your home on a 30-year mortgage, make payments biweekly. This simple strategy will help pay off a 30-year mortgage in 24 years, saving you $36,000 on a $150,000 mortgage at 6 percent. Put an additional $100 per payment and watch the savings rise further—$84,077 and the mortgage will be paid off in 17 years.

A house typically goes up in value at least by the inflation amount of 4 percent, depending on the location. Recently home prices have skyrocketed due to low interest rates. But home prices don't always go up; they are cyclical like much of our economy. When purchasing a home, find something you can buy within your cash flow and don't overcommit.

As your needs for a bigger home grow, you may be able to sell your home and transfer the equity into a larger home, or keep your home to lease out. I know several people who have successfully upgraded to newer homes every few years and leased their previous homes, which now produce a nice income.

Not everyone is cut out to be a landlord, but if you have the time and knack for this, it could pay some nice dividends and provide another source of income.

Financing a Home on a 30-Year Note

Summary

Principal Loan Balance	$150,000.00
Annual Interest Rate	6 percent
Amortization Length	30 years

Summary of Payments and Interest

Monthly Payment	$899.33
Total Interest	$173,758.80
Average Interest Each Month	$482.66

Financing a Home on a 15-Year Mortgage

Summary

Principal Loan Balance	$150,000.00
Annual Interest Rate	6 percent
Amortization Length	15 years

Summary of Payments and Interest

Monthly Payment	$1,265.79
Total Interest	$77,842.20
Average Interest Each Month	$432.46

As you can see from the comparison of a 30-year mortgage and a 15-year mortgage, the savings is huge: $95,916 difference in the interest paid. If you can afford the higher payment, consider it. However, if your budget doesn't allow for the higher repayment of a 15-year mortgage, choose the 30-year plan and add extra to your payment. This will save you thousands of dollars in interest.

Should I Pay Off My Home Before Saving for Retirement?

Some financial advisers are adamant about paying off your home mortgage before investing. I think it depends on your situation. If you are in your 30s or 40s and haven't started saving for retirement, then contribute to those plans before you pay off your mortgage, but pay extra on your home mortgage at the same time.

By contributing to IRAs and/or 401(k) plans, you can receive nice tax deductions; and you may receive a dollar-for-dollar match for some of your 401(k) or employer plan contributions.

There is no guarantee that your home values will be up if and when you need to sell your home, but reducing your home mortgage by paying extra makes good sense. If you are in your 50s and 60s and nearing retirement, focus on paying off your home mortgage before you retire, especially if you plan to live in the same home after retirement.

5

Ready, Set, Strategize

{
Know well the condition of your flock,
and pay attention to your herds
(Prov. 27:23, HCSB).
}

IN SOLOMON'S DAY, livestock was the measure of a family's wealth—whether it was sheep, cattle, goats, camels, or horses. Taking care of your livestock ensured that you had enough to cover your basic needs for living and could also yield a nice profit to buy more livestock or land.

If managed properly, you could provide your family's security for many years. Solomon's advice to know your business and take care of it is a basic element in planning.

King Solomon had the responsibility to build the Temple. This overwhelming task took seven years to complete. Did Solomon try to do it all himself? No. He appointed construction managers and hired skilled laborers. He delegated the job to experts who knew how to do it.

You cannot possibly know everything about investments, taxes, and business and estate issues. These areas can be complex and may require specialized expertise, but knowing you need to attend to them, even by delegation, is good stewardship of your resources. Today, your welfare is your work, the money you have or will have saved and invested, and any valuable assets you have accumulated. You should pay attention to your business and money so you can take care of yourself and provide for the people you love. Regularly attending to your finances will increase your chances of success.

My father, Jim Womack, was a Nazarene minister for 25 years. Most pastors don't make a big salary. Dad always said he didn't want his family to go without just because he was in ministry. He was gifted in business and provided well for us. We weren't wealthy, but we had all we needed. I remember my father saying that God likes numbers so much He named a book after it in the Bible.

If you read the Book of Numbers, you will get a taste of how much God pays attention to details. Just look at His creation; every planet strategically placed, no two humans with the same fingerprint. He has even counted the stars and named them (Ps. 147:4). I believe God expects us to know where we stand financially and to take responsibility to improve our situation.

As a financial planner, I assume most people think about doing this, but most people do not have a financial blueprint. One study I read showed that average people spend more time planning their vacations than working on their finances and future goals. No wonder so many Americans are in bad shape financially!

Can you believe that in the world's richest nation the annual median income for people 65 and older is $18,938?

More than 70 percent of people believe they won't have enough money at retirement, according to the Social Security Administration.

As a wise money manager, you will need to understand basic economic and financial concepts to help you plan for the future. Here are some to start with.

Money at Work

There are two kinds of money: *green* money and *red* money. Green money is what you save; something you preserve and can count on being there when you need it. Red money is for investing; it has few guarantees but carries a greater return potential.

You need both kinds. You need green money for your emergency fund and short-term goals. This money should be in a savings account or money market fund. The amount you allocate to the green money account depends on your stage of life, how much medical and disability coverage you have, and short-term goals.

Green Money

If you are retired, or self-employed with a sporadic income, build up the green money account to cover 3 to 6 months of living expenses. Retirees may even want 12 months saved. If you're not retired or self-employed, having 1 to 3 months of income set aside should be adequate.

Don't feel you have to have all of your short-term savings intact before starting a longer-term, red money account. Some people might need a year or longer to save one month of their income needs.

The idea is to start a green money account as soon as possible and add to it regularly. When you have a comfortable amount set aside, begin adding funds into your red money account. Remember to use the green money account only for emergencies and unexpected needs. Don't use it for normal payments. That's what your checking account is for. Without this green money account, you'll be forced into credit card debt when an emergency arises.

Types of accounts to fund your green money account with:

• Money market accounts (bank/credit union)
• Passbook savings (bank/credit union)
• Money market funds (mutual fund company)
• Ultra short-term bond funds (mutual fund company) (Ultra short-term bond funds provide a higher yield than money market and savings accounts, but they can be sensitive to interest rates and their principal can fluctuate. If you use these, put a small portion of your green money account in them.)

Ask the mutual fund company for a prospectus and review the historical return of the fund over a 5- to 10-year period. You'll want to see how the fund performed in a rising interest rate period. If you see that the total return (yield plus price of the bonds) of the fund dipped into negative territory during any of these years, stay away. Use the other accounts mentioned for your green money. The short-term bond fund may be more suitable for short-term goals and normally has a time horizon of one to three years.

Avoid spending your green money market account on unnecessary items. If you use the funds for an emergency, slowly replace the amount you've used, and resist the temptation to invest your green money into higher-risk investments.

Establish another green money account for short-term goals with a one- to three-year target date, such as: buying a new car, saving for a down payment on a home, or college. Whatever your goal is, start saving for it now.

Consider these types of accounts or investments for your short-term goals:

- Certificates of deposit
- Money market funds
- Short-term bond funds
- Exchange traded funds (ETFs that are invested in short-term corporate, government, and treasury bonds)

By planning your short-term goals and regularly allocating money to your short-term fund, you'll avoid purchasing those items on a credit card. Sticking to this system will help you enjoy the fruits of your labor and will put you in a better position for the future.

Red Money

Here are some guidelines for your red money strategy. Your red money strategy is for your goals with a time frame of three or more years. It might be for your children's college savings or to build a nest egg for your independent years.

Most of your red money will be in retirement plan savings. If your employer offers a 401(k) or other qualified plan, you'll want to join it.

The Magic of Compound Interest

Some people say the eighth wonder of the world is compound interest. Let's pretend I offered you a job that would include coming to my office seven days a week, 8 to 10 hours per day, including weekends. I would pay you one penny the first day and then double it the second day and continue to double it every day. Would you want this job?

Many people say, "No way"—but get a calculator and work through the numbers with me. The first day you would get 1 penny, the next 2 pennies, the third day 4 pennies (keep doubling for each day by hitting .01 for the first day, X 2 for day two, X 2, for day three, and so on). Your 35th day's pay alone would amount to $343,597,383! Now do you want the job?

Do you see the power of compound interest? It's truly amazing what can happen to your money over time. The rate of return you get on your money is also important. Take, for example, the illustration below of two accounts with a starting balance of $1,000; one account is earning 5 percent and the other is earning 8 percent annually:

$1,000 beginning account balance

5 Percent Rate		8 Percent Rate
$1,276	After 5 years	$1,469
$1,629	After 10 years	$2,159
$2,653	After 20 years	$4,661
$4,322	After 30 years	$10,063

What a difference a few percentage points make! After 30 years you would have almost two and a half times that amount at 8 percent, versus money saved at a 5 percent rate.

Fixed investments such as bonds, certificates of deposit, and money markets can be good investments but historically have not kept up with the cost of living. You will need to put some money in stocks, real estate, and other hard assets to earn more than the average rate of return. If you are not familiar with these investments, learn about them. Take a course, read, and seek the advice of a trusted friend, businessperson, or investment adviser.

Time is money. The more time you let your money work, the more it can do for you. Proverbs 13:11 tells us, "Dishonest money dwindles away, but he who gathers money little by little makes it grow."

Two keys are to invest regularly and be consistent. Start investing as soon as you have paid off all consumer debt (credit cards, car loans, other short-term loans). Many people don't start an investment plan until they see the perfect opportunity. That may never happen. Just start with something: $100, $50.00, or $25.00 a month. Before you know it, you'll have a nice nest egg. If you work for a company that provides a retirement plan, like a 401(k), this is the ideal place to start investing your red money. Many employer plans will match a portion of your contributions.

If you are self-employed or don't have a company plan, consider establishing an individual retirement account (IRA), a Roth IRA, or a simplified employee pension (SEP).

The Increasing Cost of Living and Living Too Long

If you had an annual income of $36,000, it may have to increase to $56,087 in 15 years to have the same purchasing power it does today. If your income of $36,000 remains level, because of inflation, in 15 years your income would be worth only $23,107 in today's dollars.

How does your dollar keep up with or exceed the cost of living? You put it to work at rates above the average inflation rate. The average inflation rate over 25 years has been 4 percent. So your money must earn at least 5 to 6 percent. After taxes and inflation your return may have to exceed 6 to 8 percent. Traditionally, people who own stocks, real estate, and other hard assets not only keep up with inflation but also exceed it. Building a diversified portfolio can reduce your risk, increase your return potential, and help keep your wealth building for future years.

The average person lives 20 years after retirement, so your investments will need to grow to provide you with an increasing income the longer you live. One of the worst fears of a retiree is outliving his or her money.

If you are fortunate to make $60,000 per year from age 35 to age 65 and your average tax rate is 20 percent, your total taxes could exceed $590,000! There are many legal ways to reduce your taxes. One of the first basic tax breaks is contributing to a retirement plan.

Most people think that they'll be in a lower tax bracket at retirement. Don't count on it. With the mounting national debt, our taxes will probably increase the next few years. Many of my retired clients pay as much in taxes now as they paid when they worked—mostly because they accumulated amounts in tax-deductible plans and must now pull money out that is subject to taxation.

If you are eligible to contribute to a Roth IRA, along with your company-sponsored plan, it will help manage your tax burden during your distribution years. Roths grow tax-free, as regular IRAs do, but when you take money out, it is tax-free.

Avoid High Risk—"Hot Tips" Will Get You Burned!

Ecclesiastes 5:13-14 says, "There is another serious problem I have seen under the sun. Hoarding riches harms the saver. Money is put into risky investments that turn sour, and everything is lost. In the end, there is nothing left to pass on to one's children" (NLT). To be a successful investor, avoid high-risk investments, especially those with no track record. A popular example is penny stocks, which are traded in over-the-counter exchanges because they are too small to be listed on the major exchanges.

Many times these companies hire public relations firms to promote them, trying to get attention by overselling their products, services, or potential market share. Basically they are trying to lure investors to load up—creating high demand in a short time, which causes the price to rise. Then the big shareholders dump the stock while small traders bid the price higher.

This is where you get burned. You can make money in penny stocks and you could lose it all—fast. Your chances are probably better in Las Vegas. Stick to a diversified portfolio of larger, established companies.

If someone offers you a deal that has a high return, no risk, tax-free, guaranteed income, stop, turn, and run! Most of your red money should be invested in companies or programs that have proven track records, sound management, and outstanding products or services.

As Solomon said, "Wealth from get-rich-quick schemes quickly disappears; wealth from hard work grows over time" (Prov. 13:11, NLT).

Avoiding high-risk investments also helps you avoid big losses. When you lose money from a bad investment, it can take months or even years to recover. This illustration shows what it takes to recover from a loss:

A Loss of . . .	Requires a Return of . . .
-25 percent	33 percent
-33 percent	50 percent
-50 percent	100 percent
-75 percent	300 percent
-90 percent	900 percent

Between 1984 and 2003 the U.S. stock market (S&P 500) grew by 12.98 percent per year. According to Dalbar, Inc., during this same period the average mutual fund investor earned only 3.51 percent.

Why did the average investor earn only 3.51 percent during America's greatest bull market? Many investors lacked a strategy. Because of a lack of strategy, investors are vulnerable to every idea that comes along and succumb to emotion-based decision-making in which greed and fear cause them to buy and sell at the worst times.

Before you invest, develop a plan.

The Wise Money Manager's Investment Checklist

1. Establish Your Goals. Why are you investing? For income? For retirement or to start a new business? If you are investing for six months to three years, you should not invest in the stock market or stock funds. Use a money market fund, certificate of deposit, or savings account.

The stock market should be for investment goals of three years or longer. If you needed the funds at a time when the markets were down, you may sell at a loss. The longer you keep money invested in the stock market, the better the chances of a positive return.

2. Evaluate Your Risk Tolerance. After you establish goals, learn to understand investment risk. Many tools can help you find the type of investments best suited for you. Find the mix of asset classes and categories that will best meet your risk level. This will help when the markets are volatile but will not guarantee against loss of principal. Your time frame will determine how aggressive you should get. If you have five years or more, you can be more aggressive than someone who will need funds sooner.

The economy and stock market face up and down market cycles, with the average economic cycle of three years. Of course, there is no guarantee of investment returns in the market, so know your aversion to market risk to better understand how it works and increase your probability of investing success.

The lower the return, the lower the risk. The higher the return potential, the more risk you'll take.

3. Diversify. Don't put all your eggs into one basket. Diversification is essential to building an investment strategy. In investment and financial planning workshops I ask participants if they think their investments are really diversified. One lady told me she was very diversified because she invested in four highly rated stock mutual funds. Later I discovered her funds had nine stock holdings repeated in the top 20 holdings within each fund. This is not exactly diversification. Even though one fund's name was identified by "value" and another by "growth," she still had similar holdings in those funds.

When you invest your money in mutual funds or other investments, loss of principal could occur. Many investors may not be as diversified as they may think. That's because traditional portfolios are comprised exclusively of stocks, bonds, and cash. While stocks and bonds may complement each other during up markets, they can move in the same direction during flat markets. So diversifying your holdings can reduce certain types of investment risk.

Understanding your funds holdings and how they can react during market cycles is important in determining your diversification. Certain types of investment asset classes react differently to each other. When one goes up the other may go down. The industry term for this is *negative correlation*. By spreading your money in different types of investments that have negative correlation to each other, you can help manage risk and potentially boost returns.

Here are a list of asset classes and their historical degree of negative correlation to each other:

Historical Correlation of Various Asset Classes vs. S&P 500
December 31, 1996—December 31, 2006

Equity Leverage Strategy	+1.00
S&P 500	+1.00
International Equity	+0.79
Long/Short	+0.58
Hedge Fund	+0.49
REITs	+0.31
Fixed Income Inverse	+0.16
Cash	+0.06
Currency	+0.03
Commodities	-0.04
Bonds	-0.11
Fixed Income Leveraged	-0.17
Managed Futures	-0.18
Equity Inverse	-0.99

As you can see, spreading your money in different stock and bond funds, including international funds, may not provide ample diversification. Look at more advanced strategies such as managed futures, commodities, and equity inverse investments.

Inverse strategies include funds managed to perform in direct reversal of the stated index. In an inverse fund, if the stock market went up 3 percent one month, the inverse fund would be down 3 percent.

The managers of these strategies buy and sell securities that move in the opposite direction of the targeted index. You naturally wouldn't want to be overly exposed to this inverse strategy during a market uptrend, but they might make sense for part of a stock portfolio when the market is down or flat. Like any investment, you should review carefully before investing.

Mutual funds are a popular way to invest, especially if you have $250,000 or less.

Here are the advantages of a mutual fund:

- **Professional Management.** Trained professionals buy and sell stocks and have the research, time, and tools to help them manage the portfolio.
- **Economical.** The fund managers can buy large quantities of a stock at a lower price than you can. You can diversify among hundreds of companies at a more competitive cost than you could do on your own.
- **Liquidity.** You can get in and out of a fund with relative ease.
- **Diversification.** Provided with the immediate benefit of instant diversification and potential asset allocation without the large amounts of cash needed to create individual portfolios.

Here are the disadvantages of mutual funds:

- **Variable Returns.** Like many investments, you have no guaranteed return, even with funds invested in U.S. treasuries. Just because you have professional management doesn't guarantee the fund will be safe or yield high returns.
- **Too Much Diversification.** While diversification is important, a fund can be so spread out that the returns are watered down. Or if the fund manager keeps too much in cash, which can happen when too many investors send in money in a short period of time, this can be a problem.
- **Cost and Fees.** Many funds have sales loads (front-end, back-end, and continuous fees), and every fund has a management fee. Read the prospectus and compare the total fee structure to similar funds in its class.

- **Not Known by Their Name.** Some funds are incorrectly labeled. While their name may have a certain style, such as value, they may invest in positions that are more aggressive and growth-oriented.

Choosing mutual funds is not easy since more than 8,000 mutual funds are available. This does not include exchange traded funds (ETFs), closed-end funds, and unit investment trusts (UITs).

Do your homework and request the fund company's prospectus and other data. Seeking a third party report on your prospective fund will help you see an unbiased view. Morningstar research firm provides good information and commentaries on the fund, its holdings, and other fundamental data.

Be sure not to pick funds only because they have performed well in the past—yesterday's big winners may be tomorrow's big losers. Look for consistency and compare the fund to its peer group or benchmark index.

Do You Need Income from Your Investments?

Here are some considerations for income-producing holdings:

Conservative income-producing investments:

- Certificates of deposit (FDIC guarantee)
- Treasury notes or T-bills (government-backed)
- Passbook savings accounts (typically insured)
- Money market funds (not insured, considered safe)
- Income annuities (backed by the paying ability of the insurance company)
- Municipal bonds and tax-free bonds (some are insured)
- Federal agency bonds (federal home loan notes)

More aggressive forms of income-producing investments:
- Corporate bonds or bond funds
- Municipal bonds (higher yielding, tax-free interest)
- Preferred stocks
- Convertible bonds
- Dividend paying stocks (real estate investment trusts, utilities, and blue chip stocks)
- Limited partnerships (real estate, oil/gas, equipment leasing)

Paying for Advice

You can invest your money in several ways: (1) no load; (2) fee-based; (3) load/commission. Here are the pros and cons of each:

1. No Load. This is where you set up an online, discount brokerage account and do your own research and trades or apply for mutual funds through a no-load fund company. Advantages: Lower trading cost and fees compared to traditional brokerage or load mutual funds. Disadvantages: Limited assistance in planning and no coordinated financial plan; cost of time spent compared to hiring an adviser.

2. Fee-Based. Hiring an adviser for a fee. Some fee-only advisers charge by the hour or by the size of account. Advantages: The adviser is compensated by fees, not by activity in the account. This keeps the adviser from trying to sell you something. Disadvantages: More advisers are moving to this style of management. You must make sure the adviser is working to earn his or her keep and providing value-added service through improved returns, reduced risk, or other planning services.

3. Load/Commission. Broker or adviser receives a commission or fees paid by the fund company or when they sell/buy stocks or other investments. Advantages: Most load fees with mutual funds are one-time only, so when you've paid for your transaction, your costs could be lower compared to a fee-based account over time. You can still find good advisers or brokers who work on a commission. If the advice and services are good, it may be just as efficient to invest this way. Disadvantages: Adviser is motivated to sell or churn an account to make a sale. Or advisers don't pay attention to the account over time because they are not paid to do so. Request the broker or adviser to disclose his or her compensation and compare it to other methods of investing.

My take: When the markets are doing great, anybody can make money. When the markets aren't doing well, you especially need direction. A good adviser should help you keep on track and provide you with value-added services to help you work toward your life goals. Unless you have the desire and time to spend several hours each week on your portfolio, you may be better served with an investment professional. When the adviser is paid an advisory fee, he or she is required as a fiduciary (a person legally appointed and authorized to hold assets in trust for another person, instead of his or her own profit) to provide you with ongoing advice and services.

The adviser should not make a commission on an investment and then charge you an advisory fee. The advisory, fee-based method requires you to sign an advisory agreement spelling out what the adviser will do.

The fees are also disclosed. Fees for this type of service will range from 2 percent to 1 percent annually depending on the account size. The higher the account value, the lower the fee. For a portfolio to typically go below a 1 percent annual fee you would have to have more than a million dollars in the account.

What should you receive for advisory services? You should at least receive a quarterly evaluation and at least one face-to-face annual review. Make sure the adviser is actually working for you and not just throwing you into a mix of funds. Make the adviser earn his or her keep.

Take some gains. When it comes to the economy and investments, there are good times and bad. Selling to take your gains every so often is smart. Consider taking gains every year, especially in tax-deferred accounts like IRAs because the taxes are deferred in retirement accounts—you don't pay taxes when you sell, only when you pull money out of the plan.

Invest the gains in areas of your portfolio that have not done as well or in areas of the economy that have experienced a downturn. Eventually, those sectors will come back, perhaps while other positions are down.

Repeat this investment strategy at least annually regardless of market conditions. The industry term for this is called *rebalancing.* For the rebalancing strategy to work, you must have a diversified allocation of various asset classes. By adding alternative investment strategies within the portfolio, you'll have some assets that may go down or not perform as well as the others. You need this for true diversification and for rebalancing to work. It's basically selling high (those assets that have done well) and buying low (into those that haven't done as well). If the markets are more volatile, consider more frequent rebalancing, perhaps every quarter or six months.

Don't follow the crowd. Sometimes we react with herd mentality—we don't want to get left behind or look odd, so we buy or do what the crowd is doing. Here is a basic rule in investing: When everyone is doing it and the headlines are full of it—it's usually too late. People tend to make investment decisions with their emotions, whether fear or greed.

When the stock market is hot and returns are above average, that's usually a sign of a market top. When everybody is scared and selling, that's typically a sign of a market bottom.

In some instances, you should invest in sectors or investment classes that everyone is selling; and sell what everyone is buying. Having an investment strategy that includes diversification will help you to not panic when the markets get ugly. It will also help you be prudent when everyone is rushing in.

A good example is the technology market top of early 2000. In the latter part of the 1990s we saw growth stocks, particularly technology, run up. A few value managers warned that the companies people wanted to purchase were priced high compared to their earnings. Some high-tech, start-up companies were not even close to making a profit.

People ignored the warnings and invested in high potential growth stocks, causing the NASDAQ composite index to rise 179 percent in two years (3/31/98 to 3/31/00). At the peak of the NASDAQ in March 2000, it stood at 5,132 points. It then proceeded to sell off and eventually bottomed at a level of 1,108 points—a 78 percent decrease. Many investors got to the party just before it ended and suffered. The NASDAQ composite has recovered from the lows but is still way off its all-time high.

It is interesting to see that the investments people avoided because of their lackluster performance during the growth surge outperformed during the growth sell-off from 2000 through 2002.

Bonds, real estate, and hard assets like gold outperformed the stock market and did exceptionally well during the stock bear market of the early 2000s. Nobody wanted these blah holdings in 1998 and 1999. Those who owned some real estate, bonds, and commodities in their portfolios fared better.

I'm not saying just because the market is doing well there aren't any opportunities, but in some of your investments, look for things that have underperformed but still have good long-term opportunity—things that won't go away.

Don't hoard it! If you are blessed and fortunate to build substantial wealth, remember what Jesus said, "It is easier for a camel to go through the eye of a needle than for a rich person to enter the Kingdom of God!" (Luke 18:25, NLT).

Put your money where your faith is. Should you care how and where your money is invested? Many mutual funds and money managers invest in companies that directly or indirectly support abortion, pornography, alternative lifestyles, anti-family values, alcohol, tobacco, and gambling.

If you choose not to invest in these kinds of companies, you'll have to research the companies' affiliations to determine if they align with God's Word and your convictions. This can be quite a task if you have a large portfolio.

A few mutual fund companies focus their efforts on social and morally responsible investing. One company is the Timothy Plan family of funds, based upon biblical stewardship principles of 1 Tim. 5:8, 22. Another company with faith-based and moral investing is the Ave Maria Fund family.

Several of these companies' funds do have historical above-average returns and have a highly rated 4- and 5-Star by Morningstar. The fees for some morally and socially conscious funds can be a little higher compared to a traditional mutual fund.

Your money is an extension of your values as it works through the economy. Should you care about where your money goes and what it represents? Here are a few scriptures to consider:

- "Do not be unequally yoked with unbelievers. For what partnership has righteousness with lawlessness? Or what fellowship has light with darkness?" (2 Cor. 6:14, ESV).
- "Do not enter the path of the wicked, and do not walk in the way of the evil" (Prov. 4:14, ESV).
- "Treasures gained by wickedness do not profit, but righteousness delivers from death" (10:2, ESV).
- "Better is a little with righteousness than great revenues with injustice" (16:8, ESV).

Self-Evaluation

What areas of money management am I good at? _____

_____

What areas do I need help with? _____

_____

What are two steps I can take to manage my money more effectively?

1. _____

2. _____

Can I manage my investments, or do I need an adviser?

_____

Sometimes Life Doesn't Make Sense

I'm sure you've seen successful people who don't honor God. Why do godless people seem to make all the money? A tip from Solomon:

I have observed something else under the sun. The fastest runner doesn't always win the race, and the strongest warrior doesn't always win the battle. The wise sometimes go hungry, and the skillful are not necessarily wealthy. And those who are educated don't always lead successful lives. It is all decided by chance, by being at the right place at the right time (*Eccles. 9:11, NLT*).

Just keep doing what you know is right. Be consistent and leave the rest to God. It's in His hands.

6

Your Financial Map
Charting Your Course

HAVE YOU EVER TAKEN A ROAD TRIP? Did you throw
your stuff in the car and just take off? Did you make sure you
had enough money for gas, food, and lodging? What about
the car? Did you check the tire pressure, belts, and fluids? To
make your trip less stressful and more successful, a road map
will also come in handy. On the Internet, you can get directions showing every turn and what roads to take. This map
may even show you how many miles and hours it will take to
complete the trip.

Armed with this information, you can calculate how much
gas you'll need and how many stops for food, fuel, and
overnight stays (and where you'll stop) you'll need, but the
key in getting your online directions is entering a starting
point—noting where you are right now.

Many people travel through life with an idea of where they
would like to be, but with no real direction. They stop along
the way asking for directions, getting different advice on how

to make it to their destination. If they would only get printed directions to the destination, they could enjoy the trip more.

Likewise, you need a money map that will give directions to your financially independent years. You need to know how long it will take you and what it will cost. This money map should be updated regularly to help you stay on track and avoid pitfalls that stand ready to detour your progress. Roadblocks, detours, and traffic jams are all part of life, but by preparing for them, you will be able to make necessary adjustments and continue toward your goals.

Your money map should address the following areas of planning:

- How much cash savings you need
- Protecting your assets and your family from various risks
- Avoiding or reducing costly debt
- Minimizing your tax burden
- Preparing for your children's education
- Allocating savings for your independent years
- Diversifying your investment portfolio to minimize risk and earn a competitive return
- A written plan to pass your estate to your heirs; leaving your legacy

Set Your Sights

Where do you want to be in 10 years, 20 years, or even 30 years? At what age do you want to become financially independent so you don't need to work? What income do you want to get you through your independent years; and do you want to leave an inheritance to your children, grandchildren, or your favorite charity?

These goals are your final destination plans. The moment you start working, the clock starts ticking toward your goals. Just because you're young doesn't mean you don't need to plan or save. The earlier you start, the sooner you'll reach your destination and the more freedom you'll have when you get there.

If you have waited to plan, you still have time. This exercise will help you evaluate your current planning. You may need to write your answers on another piece of paper.

Cash Management

I have enough cash in liquid savings to equal at least one month of my living expenses.   ☐ Yes   ☐ No

What can you do to improve your liquid savings? _____

_____

I have adequate insurance to protect my assets and loved ones.   ☐ Yes   ☐ No

What areas of risk management do you need to address? (property, liability, health, income protection, life insurance, long-term care insurance, identity theft and fraud protection)

_____

I have eliminated or am reducing consumer debts.
☐ Yes   ☐ No

What can I do to free myself from creditors? _____

_____

I have taken advantage of all applicable tax reduction strategies.   ☐ Yes   ☐ No

Am I satisfied with the amount of my tax? What areas

could benefit from tax planning? _____

_____

    I have made plans for my children's or grandchildren's education and started an investment fund for them.
☐ Yes   ☐ No

    I am familiar with the Education IRA, the 529 College Savings Plan, the Uniform Gifts to Minors Act (UGMA) Account, and other ways to save for them.   ☐ Yes   ☐ No

    I know the amount I need to reach my financial independence goals and am currently saving toward this goal.
☐ Yes   ☐ No

    If retired, I have projected my future living expenses.
☐ Yes   ☐ No

    My investments are diversified to meet my level of risk and my objectives.   ☐ Yes   ☐ No

    Based on my age and objectives, I feel my portfolio is _____

_____

    Too much risk, or not enough, can impact my investment. With this in mind, is my portfolio too risky or not risky enough? _____

_____

    I have a written plan that allows my estate to pass efficiently to my heirs.   ☐ Yes   ☐ No

    What areas of estate planning do I need information on to formulate a better plan? _____

_____

    Are there special areas—such as charitable giving, providing for someone's special needs, or business planning strategies—that need attention? If so, what? _____

_____

On the planning items mentioned, which do I need professional help with? _____

_____

Who can help with my concerns? _____

_____

Set a date to follow up on your planning concerns and
contact someone for help. _____

Your Destination: Independence!

You may spend over a third of your life working—for
what? Most of us want the opportunity to do what we enjoy,
whenever we want, with whom we want—financial freedom!

This is a worthwhile goal, and depending on the lifestyle
you desire, it probably won't happen by accident. Many Web
sites offer financial calculators to help you. Your financial
planner can also help project your needs. But several assump-
tions can alter your projections:

- Amount of income you'll need during your lifetime and
  how long you'll need it—your longevity
- The number of years you have to reach your independence
- The growth rate on your savings during the accumula-
  tion phase and for the distribution phase
- Inflation rate for annual cost of living increases throughout your lifetime
- Other income sources such as Social Security, pension
  income, and wages

- Additional considerations: health-care costs, inheritance, and charitable bequests

Income Needs

There are two common methods to help you determine how much income you will need during your independence years: replacement ratio and estimated expenses.

The replacement ratio method uses a percentage of your preretirement income to estimate how much you'll need. The ratio of replacement could range from 70 to 90 percent. The percentage you need will depend upon how much income you use for the replacement amount. For example, the larger a person's income, the smaller the replacement ratio he or she may need. The smaller income may require a similar income during the retirement years and could be 80 to 90 percent of preretirement income. This method is preferred for people who are 20 years from retirement.

The estimated expense method will provide a more accurate picture of income needs and is derived by calculating annual expenses on an item-by-item source. This will let you use more accurate numbers when estimating your income needs for housing, entertainment, food, medical care, utilities, taxes, and other items. This method is preferred for those who are closer to retirement because it is based upon current expenses.

Whatever your amount of annual income need, it should be in today's dollar amounts without inflation. You'll use an inflation factor later to get a future value.

Other considerations for income needs include mortgage balance during retirement, travel and vacations, possible lower taxes, reduced savings budget, and dependents to support.

Once you have determined your estimated annual income

need for your independence years, determine how long you may need the income. Thanks to improved lifestyle habits and medical advances, we live longer, healthier lives. Centenarians are the fastest growing age-group in America. The Census Bureau predicts the nation could have more than 1 million by 2050, up from 71,000 today. According to *USA Today*, in 2046, there could be 79 million baby boomers between the ages of 82 to 100.

This will put tremendous pressure on our nation's healthcare and retirement benefit systems, as well as on you to provide your own long-term financial security. You should plan to make your money last as long as you might—and that could be age 90 or older. This means if you retire at age 65, you'll need to make your money last for 25 years or longer!

Next, list savings, investments, and retirement plan balances that you have set aside for your independence years. If you have at least 10 years or more to save for your retirement, consider a diversified stock portfolio of mutual funds and other managed futures. These asset categories outperform bonds and fixed income investments and have kept above the average inflation rate over the years.

Although the stock market has performed over 10 percent annualized returns for the past 50 years, this doesn't mean it will continue to do so in the future. What would happen if you planned on the markets making 10 percent but ended up only averaging 7 percent? A 3 percent difference over 20 years is huge. This is why I encourage clients to project no more than an 8 percent average annual (pretax) return during their working years, and then reduce this rate to at least 6 percent during their distribution phase.

You will now need to project the future value of your income needs to allow for inflation. In mainstream economics, the word *inflation* refers to a general rise in prices measured against a standard level of purchasing power. There are many measures of inflation depending on the circumstances. The most well known are the CPI (consumer price index), which measures consumer prices, and the GDP (gross domestic product) deflator, which measures inflation in the economy.

We have been spoiled over the last 10 years by having an annual inflation rate of 2.54 percent. However, if you take a longer-term view, say over the past 30 years, the annualized inflation rate in the U.S. has been 4.68 percent—almost double that of the last 10 years.

To put this in terms of purchasing power, it would take $5.19 in the year 2006 to have the same purchasing power as $1.00 did in 1970. Project this same rate of inflation into the future and you will need $26.94 in 2036 to have the same purchasing power as $5.19 today. (See www.measuring worth.com)

The inflation rate usually varies in cycles, with periods of high inflation following periods of lower inflation. Could we be in for higher inflationary times? Due to our nation's current debt, trade imbalance, and easy-money fiscal policies of the last few years, I believe we can expect to see higher inflation maybe even exceeding the last 30 years. So use a 4 or 5 percent inflation rate to project your income needs.

Other Income Sources

List all your fixed sources of income separate from your retirement savings and personal investments. The first source to consider is Social Security. One-third of Americans over 65 depend on Social Security benefits for 90 percent of their income. With the aging of America, this will drastically change over the next 30 years. Here is a potential glimpse of our social insecurity:

- In 1950, 16 workers supported every one Social Security beneficiary compared to 3.3 workers today.
- In 2008 baby boomers will begin to retire. Over the next few decades, people will live longer and benefits will increase. By the time today's youngest workers turn 65, only 2 workers will support each beneficiary.
- Under the current system, today's 30-year-old worker will face a 27 percent benefit cut when he or she reaches retirement.
- In 2017 the government will pay out more in Social Security benefits than it collects in payroll taxes, and shortfalls will grow larger with each year.
- By 2027 the government will have to find an extra $200 billion a year to keep the system afloat.
- By 2033 the annual shortfall will be more than $300 billion.
- By 2041 the system will be bankrupt.

(See www.whitehouse.gov/infocus/social-security)

To save Social Security for the future, experts tell us major changes will occur. Bottom line: Don't depend on Social Security as a significant resource for your independence years, especially if you are younger than 40.

Just because things look bleak doesn't mean you shouldn't plan around it; you will just need to adjust your planning as the changes occur. If you use Social Security as a projected income source, factor in a lower cost of living increase for those benefits.

For example, if your income needs to increase by 4 percent per year, estimate your Social Security benefits increasing by only 2 percent to 3 percent per year. This may make your retirement projection more realistic considering the uncertainty of the Social Security system.

Every worker who is not receiving Social Security benefits should be receiving an annual benefits statement. It is important to review these and confirm the amount of income on your records. If you see a discrepancy, contact the Social Security Administration. You can access more information on Social Security from the government's Web site at <http://www.ssa.gov/>. Here you can calculate your benefits, apply for benefits, and request a benefit statement.

Many retirees plan to work during their independence years—whether to supplement income or to begin a new career. As Americans live longer, healthier lives, many will need extra income. But remember, if you plan to receive Social Security benefits before you reach the full retirement age (FRA), your benefits will be reduced by $1.00 for every $2.00 earned (wages) over the exemption amount.

For 2007, you can earn $12,960 and not be affected—any earnings above this would be reduced by $1.00 for every $2.00 above this exemption.

When should you decide to take retirement benefits?

- If you have not reached your full retirement age (FRA) and are still earning substantial income, it is generally not to your advantage to begin benefits.
- If you retire before reaching your FRA, you may need to receive benefits to meet your current living expenses. Benefits may be partially tax-free and may allow you to

delay drawing income from assets that are growing on a tax-deferred basis.

- If you do not need Social Security to meet your current living expenses, consider delaying benefits until you reach your FRA or beyond, and receive larger benefits. Or take your benefits and invest them in a personal account or establish a deferred gifting strategy that will let you make tax-deductible contributions, receive a future income, and benefit a charity upon your death. You can find many creative ways to use your retirement benefits if you do not need the monthly income.

Health care is another good reason to wait until the FRA before stopping work. At your FRA (age 67 for those born after 1960) you can use Medicare, which covers many medical care costs. Until then, unless you retire from a corporation that pays retirees' medical insurance, it may be cost prohibitive to get insurance coverage on your own. I work with many clients who retired before the FRA, took reduced Social Security benefits, and worked just enough to pay for their health care until they qualified for Medicare.

Fidelity predicted that a couple retiring in 2007 without health-care benefits would need $215,000 for medical costs during retirement. That doesn't include the cost of over-the-counter medications, dental services, and long-term care.

Employee Benefit Research Institute last year estimated that costs would be even higher. A couple, it said, should expect to spend $295,000 for health-care premiums and out-of-pocket expenses during retirement.

Dallas Salisbury, president of EBRI in Washington, D.C., said, "The public overwhelmingly thinks that Medicare covers all retiree medical expenses." About 80 percent of people, he said, think it covers long-term care, which it doesn't. Medicare, according to EBRI, covers only about half of retiree health expense.

Consumers should expect to spend about $125 a month for individual coverage and $250 for a couple, said Cara Jareb, director of retiree medical consulting for Watson Wyatt.

Determine how much you might spend on health-care expenses, including insurance. Also consider the costs of long-term care insurance. The national average cost for a private room in a nursing home is $70,912 a year. For in-home assistance, the national average cost is $22.15 per hour, or $46,072 per year for 40 hours of help per week.

These costs will only increase. At a 5 percent inflation rate, a year in a nursing home could cost more than $110,008 in 2015 and $179,191 in 2025. The cost of in-home care could be more than $71,473 in 2015 and almost $116,422 in 2025.

7

Diversify

Divide your investments among many places,
for you do not know what risks might
lie ahead *(Eccles. 11:2, NLT)*.

WHILE MUCH UNCERTAINTY surrounds the future of our economy, opportunities will probably also occur. So here are some ideas on trends that may dramatically affect your future or that of your children and grandchildren. Many of these opportunities will come as a result of the world's demographic trends.

According to the U.S. Census Bureau, in America, the number of people age 65 and older is projected to double from 36 million to 72 million in 2030, and increase from 12 percent to 20 percent of the population.

Last summer I heard Jeremy J. Siegel, professor of finance at the Wharton School of the University of Pennsylvania, speak about his recent book, *The Future for Investors*. In the book he devoted several chapters to the coming age wave, the challenges it could bring to our world economy and standard of living, and some possible solutions. He pointed out that as badly off as the United States is in facing future projections, "Most European countries and Japan are in worse shape and have pension obligations that are far greater."[1]

He made a further point that as people retire by the masses, who will they sell their stock investments to in order to turn them into cash or generate income? The market will probably be flooded with those who need to sell without enough people in the system to buy. If you can't sell your stocks, they're worthless.

Doesn't sound encouraging, does it? Fortunately Siegel suggests the developing countries of the world don't have age problems and will potentially own most of the wealth the larger developed countries now enjoy. They may buy the securities from the older generation. Dr. Siegel does see the glass as half full. That's encouraging.

When considering the effects of the coming age wave and the growth of developing countries, let's look at the demands this phenomenon will have on resources and services:

- **Health Care.** Health care will benefit from the graying of America. The increased need for nursing homes, extended care facilities, retirement villages, and medical equipment—all could point to increased demand for the health-care sector.

- **Technology.** According to forecasts, the worldwide Internet population is over 1 billion and will reach 2 billion by 2011. Broadband subscribers will reach 400 million by 2010. New ways to communicate and entertain are created almost daily, and the demand for computer security and storage is escalating.

- **Financial Companies.** Banks, insurance, and investment companies should benefit from baby boomers maximizing their retirement savings and planning for retirement years.

- **Natural Resources and Commodities.** Global growth, especially from emerging economies like China, India, and Brazil, will continue to drive the demand for natural resources higher. Chemicals, building materials, energy, forest products, agriculture and metals, and mining companies may benefit from a growing global economy.

  According to the International Energy Agency, worldwide oil consumption was projected to 85 million barrels per day. Natural gas consumption will increase from 65 billion cubic feet per day (BCFD) to 85 BCFD over the next decade. The technology to create clean water is already a booming business. Add the demands of an increasing global population and this natural resource is second only to oil. China alone estimates it will need to invest $241 billion by 2010 to improve distribution and quality of water.

  Commodities have historically been a great way to diversify investment portfolios. During flat periods of the U.S. stock market between 1966 and 1982, commodity markets boomed.

- **Alternative Energy.** Supply disruptions, political instability, and a decline in oil production will drive the need for energy alternatives. Many companies will focus their efforts on new ways to meet energy demands. President Bush has proposed initiatives to increase clean-energy research by 22 percent, and he proposed a goal of replacing 75 percent of U.S. oil imports from the Middle East by 2025. Hybrid vehicles are becoming more affordable. Hydrogen-powered vehicles are gaining feasibility. Ethanol is becoming a viable energy source.

- **Homeland Security and Defense.** Protecting our homeland will continue to be a concern. Companies will invest in technologies to safeguard physical and intellectual property.

- **International Stocks.** Large U.S. companies with a substantial market share outside of the U.S. should do well. The economies of developing nations are predicted to grow faster than those of developed ones.

For the stock portion of a growth portfolio, I would suggest:

Core Holdings

40 percent	Lifestyle or target date funds
20 percent	International fund of funds
40 percent	Strategic alpha portfolio

With 5 percent to 10 percent in the following sectors or themes:

- Global Natural Resources
- Homeland Security/Defense
- Health Care
- Technology
- Alternative Energy
- Water Utility
- Financials

You should rebalance the strategic alpha portfolio at least annually, especially in tax-sheltered accounts like IRAs. This will give you opportunity to take gains in the winners and reinvest at lower prices on sectors that don't perform well.

Rebalancing requires selling securities at a gain, which will be taxable if investments are in a nonretirement account. If the asset is sold in less than 12 months, it is considered short-term for any gains and taxed at ordinary income tax rates (highest of 35 percent). Long-term gains (held at least 12 months) are taxed at the maximum rate of 15 percent.

Bottom line: Rebalance at least annually in tax-sheltered accounts or more frequently during periods of market volatility. Consider rebalancing taxable accounts every 13 months so any gains are taxed at the lower, long-term capital gain rate.

For the strategic alpha portfolio, consider sector funds or exchanged traded funds (ETF) that focus on the particular area. Managed mutual funds can be good choices for the sectors. However, with traditional mutual funds you have the tax issue of short- and long-term capital gains that can frequently be paid to shareholders. Therefore, they may be fine for your tax-sheltered plans but not very tax-efficient for your nonretirement account. ETFs can be much more tax-efficient compared to a mutual fund.

I also find that unit investment trusts (UITs) can fund the sectors efficiently. UITs are a nonmanaged basket of securities that are held until a specified maturity date. Usual terms range from 2 to 10 years, depending on the trust. At the end of the UIT term, the trust is liquidated and any gains are realized. Then you can reinvest the proceeds.

If held to expiration, any gains would be taxed as long-term gains. Because UITs are not managed, they have a low fee structure compared to most mutual funds and ETFs.

Keeping It Simple

Lifestyle or target date funds can be a great way to diversify your holdings if you want a simple approach. These are based on your age, risk level, and time horizon. They also can be pegged for a certain retirement date (i.e., if you were 50 years of age in 2007 and wanted to retire at age 65 you would choose the Target 2022 Fund for your target retirement date in 2022). As you get closer to your retirement date, the fund will automatically adjust to be more conservative by adding fixed income, money markets, and more conservative equity exposure.

For younger investors choosing a longer target or time horizon, these funds will allocate more to equity stock funds of domestic and world growth and less to fixed income and money markets. These funds are usually rebalanced annually to help keep the allocation constant. This is a great way to use a core holding with a hands-off approach. You can then build your satellite holdings around this core strategy.

The Glass Half-Empty

While the future reveals potential for opportunity in the investment world, there is also an equal potential for uncertainty in the world and U.S. securities markets. Many factors could adversely affect your investments and financial security, including terrorist threats, an uncertain economy, corporate scandals, bankruptcies, hedge fund defaults, the value of the U.S. dollar, wars, and political concerns.

The U.S. economy is tough—we have persevered through many hard times. But what if something like 9/11 were to happen again on a grander scale? It would be hard to imagine the effect on our economy, our communications, our transportation system, our government, and our way of life. Even though we don't like to think about it, others look for the opportunity to wreak havoc on our way of life; unfortunately, it's just a matter of time.

We also have to think about our financial course as a nation. We are at a greater risk from a fiscal crisis than at any other time since the great depression. Our debt is at $8.9 trillion and growing $1.97 billion a day. (See zfacts.com)

If every man, woman, and child in America were to pay for our national debt, it would cost $29,493 each! If Bill Gates started paying for the national debt, at the rate it is increasing per day, he'd be broke in less than one month! We're basically spending our way into bankruptcy with our entitlement programs.

As America's population continues to gray, the Social Security, Medicare, and prescription drug programs are predicted to bankrupt our nation in the next few decades. This doesn't include grafting millions of illegal immigrants into our social system.

Warren Buffett recently pointed out in *Financial Intelligence Report,* "We have gone from being a country that owned more of the rest of the world than they owned of us to the country that probably is about $3 trillion in the hole right now in terms of our net-worth position. It will have an effect, it may be a month from now, it may be five years from now, who knows, but it is not without consequences."

Monkeys Throwing Darts

Another problem I see is the investment hype in the marketplace. You can watch television shows on how to make mad money buying stocks. Hundreds of companies sell their software claiming how easy it is to make money. This is the hype you see when the markets become too loaded with small investors. Even a monkey throwing darts could make money in a hyped-up market. I'm not saying it's the end of the stock market world, but it reminds me of the tech bubble of March 2000 that caused one of the worst stock bear markets in 50 years.

Since the October 2002 bottom on the S&P 500 Index, we have not seen a healthy price decline of more than 5 percent. Based on historical trends, we are overdue. This doesn't mean we won't find opportunity for investments, but we will need to be choosy and diversify portfolios for the long term.

As Good as Gold!

Solomon said, "Wisdom is better than gold" (Prov. 16:16, RSV), but after that, gold would be a close second! Gold has been a precious metal for thousands of years. We find evidence of gold dating back to 2600 B.C. It is a highly sought precious metal, which, for many centuries, has been used as money, a store of value, and in jewelry.

Gold is the most malleable and ductile metal—a single gram can be beaten into a sheet of one square meter, or an ounce into 300 square feet. Gold is used for many things in our world: restorative dentistry; thread; as a coloring agent in glass; for electrical wiring, to name just a few.

The Bible refers to gold more than 400 times. God instructed Moses to make much of the Tent of Meeting from gold. Solomon was to laden the Temple with gold and other metals and precious stones. In Rev. 21:18, heaven is described as "the city of pure gold, as pure as glass"; and "the great street of the city was of pure gold, like transparent glass" (v. 21).

If gold is that important to us and to God, why don't we see gold as the symbol of wealth today? The U.S. dollar has symbolized wealth around the world for 30 years. But since 1971 the U.S. government removed its currency off the gold standard, and the value of the U.S. dollar has steadily declined. If our country or world hits another bad economic period, gold (and perhaps silver) should be a better investment than paper money and investments (stocks).

Owning gold and other precious metals can help provide diversification within a portfolio and provide a hedge against inflation and a global economic downturn. While the price of gold has increased, it still has room to run.

Some economists and investment gurus like Jim Rogers, cofounder of the Quantum Fund and creator of the Rogers International Commodities Index (RICI), believe we are entering a long-term boom for commodities and natural resources. According to a recent article in *Mining Weekly Online,* global gold production fell to a 10-year low in 2006.

Many world governments see the trend and are reversing their practice of selling off their gold reserves. When you combine high demand with lower supplies, this represents a strong argument for any good investment—especially one that has tremendous intrinsic value.

Buying Your Pot of Gold!

Gold Bullion

You can own gold in basically two ways today. Gold bullion is the most tangible way. You typically will buy gold coins to store for long-term and for a self-protective position against inflation and as a currency substitute. The more popular coins to buy are the American Eagles, Canadian Maple Leafs, and South African Krugerrands. To buy or sell your bullion, contact larger precious metals dealers to get pricing. You can store them in your safety deposit box or another secure location. Some brokerage firms will let you store them in your account for a nominal custodian fee.

Mining Company Stocks

You can purchase stock in companies that are involved with exploring and mining gold. Although this is not direct ownership in precious metal, it does let you participate in the movement of gold prices. There are more established senior stocks and others in smaller companies that are more speculative plays called junior stocks. The risk factors of investing in individual stocks include not only the price movement of gold but also the specific risks inherent in all companies. Many of the senior gold stock companies will also pay a dividend, which can enhance the long-term performance.

Gold mutual funds are a diversified portfolio of gold stocks that may hold senior and junior mining stocks. The mutual fund approach can be an effective way to diversify from specific company risk without banking on one or two stocks. Gold mutual funds tend to follow gold prices but will also reflect the management and performance of the underlying stock prices within the portfolio.

For as little as $500 or $1,000 you can diversify in a portfolio of gold stocks. Some of the gold funds will also invest in companies that mine other metals, such as silver and copper. Read the prospectus and annual report for a listing of stock holdings, and compare the fund's objectives, risks, and expenses with other gold stock funds.

Gold ETFs are a publicly traded stock that tracks the price of gold. The fund does not invest directly into gold stocks. It is more of a play on the price of gold versus a gold mutual fund. Currently two gold ETFs trade on the exchanges: the symbol for the streetTRACKS Gold Trust is GLD and trades on the NYSE, the other is the iShares COMEX Gold Trust with the symbol IAU, which trades on the AMEX.

To help diversify your gold-related holdings, consider the following:

- One-third in gold bullion—to store long-term
- One-third in gold stocks or gold mutual funds—for speculation, taking profits over time
- One-third in gold ETFs—for speculation, taking profits over time

Hold at least 10 percent of your overall investment portfolio in gold-related investments under normal economic conditions. Based on the current national debt and the potential crisis for our dollar, more than 10 percent may be wise.

If you want to buy gold for the long term and have a pure gold investment, consider purchasing gold bullion in one of the popular gold coins. Purchase at least one-third of your gold-related positions in gold stocks. If you are experienced in buying individual stocks and have enough to diversify in several senior companies, purchase these gold stocks for price potential. If you do not have experience researching and trading, or you don't have the time for it, consider purchasing gold mutual funds for the gold stock portion of your portfolio.

Consider purchasing the gold ETF for the rest of your

gold-related portfolio. You can trade the ETF shares frequently, and they are more liquid than mutual funds. Remember the gold ETF is tied directly to the movement of gold prices.

A Note of Caution: Have a strategy for purchasing and managing your gold portfolio. Store and preserve your bullion. For your gold stocks or funds and your gold ETFs, consider dollar cost averaging when you want to add a large position. Gold prices can be volatile, and gold, like any other investment, will undergo price trends. When buying gold stocks or ETFs, look at a chart and determine the price trend and identify support levels in the price. If the price of gold shoots up for a number of days, don't chase it right away. Most investments that shoot up quickly in a short time will go through some profit taking; wait for a pullback when traders are taking profit and then slowly add to your position.

A good rule to follow: Rebalance your gold-related stocks (only the ETFs and gold stocks or funds) with your overall investment portfolio. This means you will take gains from those investments that did well for the year and purchase or bring it back to the original allocation. Basically, sell high in areas that have moved up, and buy lower on those that have gone down.

A Silver Lining!

Silver is another precious metal that has been used as currency and is a symbol of wealth. It's mentioned in the Bible more than 300 times. The use of silver is even vaster, and it's been called the indispensable metal. Silver and silver compounds are used in many forms, such as jewelry and silverware, photography, and various industrial applications, including electronics, batteries, alternative medicines, and foods. Silver is also highly effective in antibacterial and antivirus uses.

Because of its high demand in industrial use and as currency, silver could be a worthy investment and hold its value. According to the Silver Institute, demand has steadily increased at a stronger rate compared to current production and supplies. Because there are fewer supplies above ground and such high demand for the metal, it has the potential for long-term appreciation. Silver may be "as good as gold!"

To further diversify your investment holdings, have some silver with your gold portfolio. How much depends on your exposure to gold and your overall equity holdings.

The key to investing is not losing money. To help in this goal, diversify.

Self-Evaluation

Are my investment holdings adequately diversified? _____

_____

What areas of investing do I need help with? _____

_____

What steps can I take to gain control over my investing and future security? _____

_____

8

Home, Sweet Home

{ Do your planning and prepare your fields before
building your house *(Prov. 24:27, NLT)*. }

BUYING A HOME is one of the greatest financial investments
we make. Consider the following case study involving two different buyers, both purchasing a home with the same lending
conditions.

These situations are based on interest-only, adjustable-rate
mortgages. The interest rate is 6 percent. The principal is
$100,000. The loan is a 5/1 ARM (fixed for the first five years
and adjustable every year after). The loan is also interest-only
for the first five years. All of the figures are based on principal
and interest.

Buyer No. 1: Buyer Bob is a proud father of 18-year-old
Sally, who is attending college out of state. Because of high
dorm costs, Buyer Bob purchased a three-bedroom home for
Sally, renting two rooms to her friends.

Buyer Bob decided on the above loan because his payment
would be only $500 per month versus the fully amortized

payment of $599.56. By charging the other girls $300 per month, Buyer Bob had his interest-only payment paid in full while pocketing $100 per month.

After four years, Sally graduated. Buyer Bob sold his investment home with enough equity to cover his closing costs. Buyer Bob paid off his interest-only adjustable rate mortgage before the loan became adjustable and before his payment stopped being interest-only. Buyer Bob was as proud of himself as he was of Sally.

Buyer No. 2: Buyer Bill thought he would do the same thing as Buyer Bob but for a different reason. Buyer Bill wanted a bigger home for his growing family while he finished working on his graduate degree. Buyer Bill knew he would either be moving or be able to afford the same loan fully amortized and fixed due to the potential increase in his income after graduate school. If things didn't work out, he would simply sell the home and use the equity to cover the costs.

But Buyer Bill didn't consider the possibility of increasing interest rates and a slowing market. The property values of homes declined, and interest rates increased. Buyer Bill was about to lose his adjustable rate as well as his interest-only status.

Buyer Bill became Seller Bill and couldn't find a buyer willing to pay enough to cover what he owed—not to mention the closing costs. He also couldn't refinance his home for what he owed because of its declined value. His once $500 a month payment became $733.76 a month.

Unfortunately, as Bill's interest rate rose, the increases were based on the full loan amount because no principal was paid. His payment also increased because his loan amount was fully amortized. What could have been $599.56 for the life of the loan now became $733.76 and would probably increase each year as interest rates rose.

Bill's new job awaited him in another state that he couldn't afford to move to because he couldn't pay rent there and maintain his mortgage. In fact, Bill could no longer afford his mortgage. In time, he was three months behind and facing foreclosure, something he had never considered.

Part of the American dream means owning your home. After all, it does make more sense to own than rent. When buying a house, do your homework, shore up your credit, and purchase one that will not strain your budget.

Make sure it's a buyer's market when buying; you'll build equity much quicker. The location of real estate is everything. Ask yourself what the neighborhood will look like in 10 years. What are the growth prospects? Be patient and wait for the right home and price.

When we purchased our first home, the housing market had declined and we purchased when prices were low, without even knowing what we were doing. When we sold our home 14 years later it had appreciated 75 percent. We used that equity (tax-free) to purchase a larger home.

Purchasing a home has many tax advantages and can be the cornerstone of your wealth building, but don't buy a home assuming it will be a major nest egg for your retirement years. Real estate, like other investments, can do well over time, but the recent appreciation in home prices does not indicate long-term trends in residential real estate.

Until recently the U.S. housing market was on a major bull run. With mortgage interest dropping to historical lows and mortgage companies freely lending money, real estate prices in some areas doubled.

Many people don't realize that even though real estate might be a good investment, it encounters up-and-down cycles just like the stock market. If you buy when real estate prices are high, you should be prepared to stay put awhile if the value is worth more than you paid. As you pay down the mortgage and property values rise, so does your equity.

It's not what you *paid* for your home but what you are *paying* for it. The way you finance your home can make a major difference in its equity.

You can choose from many types of mortgages today, so be sure you find one that fits your budget and will help you reduce your long-term costs so you can build equity faster. When interest rates are low, it's usually a good idea to lock in the rate for a longer period.

One problem we see today is that during the real estate boom, many interest-only loans were made for new homes, letting the homeowner keep monthly payments low by paying only the interest each month. Low payments, only for a year, gave the homeowner false security. In this situation, the payment will rise significantly. The homeowner is between a rock and a hard place, can't make the payment, then defaults.

Many subprime mortgage lenders (companies that make loans to people with poor credit) now pay the price of taking on risky mortgages. According to recent reports from the Mortgage Bankers Association, mortgage foreclosures are at record highs, and late payments rose 4.95 percent during the last quarter of 2006. This unwinding of the residential real estate market may take some time; at some point it may be compared to the dot-com collapse that brought down the stock markets for three years.

If you purchased a home in the last few years, don't panic. Hopefully you purchased to stay put for a few years. If you are in a good area, the housing market will probably calm down, find a bottom, and begin normal recovery. The key to purchasing a home is like any other investment:

- **Consider the Housing Market in Your Area.** Is it a buyer's market or a seller's market? If a bulk of inventory is on the market and houses aren't selling, it may be a good time to buy. Most Realtors say if homes are on the market more than four to six months, it's a buyer's market. If on the other hand, homes sell fast, it's a seller's market. Depending on the area of the country where you live, it still may make more sense to buy instead of paying rent and waiting for prices to drop.

- **What Are Your Goals for the House?** How long do you plan to live there? If not for at least three to five years, it may not be worth the closing costs, interest charges, and other transaction fees.

- **Don't Buy More than You Can Afford.** Consider many factors when determining how much home to buy. You want something that will fit your budget and not cramp your lifestyle. Look for your house payment, including taxes, not to exceed 30 percent of your income. Depending on your area, you may be able to reduce this to 25 percent of your annual gross income.

Another rule of thumb is to consider a home that would cost approximately two and one-half times your gross annual salary. Having a good credit rating and a low debt-to-income ratio will give you some room to work beyond this number. If you have a young family, buy with room to grow into it but also plan to move as your needs grow.

- **Borrow on Your Terms.** If interest rates are low, consider locking in the rate for the term of mortgage. Don't be tempted by interest-only or initially low rates that will creep up on you. Consider a 15-year mortgage versus a 30-year. You may have a higher payment, but you will build equity faster and save thousands of dollars in interest.

Home-Free, Tax-Free

Home ownership has many tax benefits. You can deduct the interest you pay each year from your income taxes. Licensed ministers can double-dip by deducting mortgage interest and claiming a reasonable portion of their income as housing allowance, which is excluded from the income for tax purposes.

When you sell your home, you can exclude up to $250,000 of the gain in profit if you're single or up to $500,000 if you're married. You can transfer the equity tax-free, within limits, to a new home if you meet all the guidelines.

Here are some general rules surrounding Internal Revenue Code (IRC) 121:

- You must own the home two out of five years before the sale and must have used it as a personal residence.
- If you used the home for less than two years, you may get a partial exclusion for special situations like natural disasters, change in jobs, divorce, legal separation, or multiple births from the same pregnancy.

- This tax break can be used once every 24 months.

You'll also want to keep records of home improvements, as these will add to your cost basis. If you have gains on the sale of your home, seek advice from a tax professional.

Helpful resource: Publication 523 (2006), Selling Your Home <http://www.irs.gov/publications/p523/index.html>.

Tapping into Your Home Equity

The equity you build in your home can be substantial over the years. As you pay down the mortgage and the value increases, so does your equity. One effect that led to this recent real estate bubble was the availability of easy money. Homeowners could use the equity in their homes to borrow at low rates and use that money to consolidate debts, remodel, invest, or spend it however they desired.

Borrowing to use as leverage can make good business sense. However, the abuse of borrowing can harm your financial health. I do not favor debt consolidation borrowing because it gives the borrower a false sense of security. Unless the borrower is disciplined, he or she usually ends up worse after debt consolidation.

Since your home is the cornerstone of your wealth building, don't put it in harm's way. Use the equity only as a last resort and repay as soon as possible. Don't get caught up in the old excuse, "It's tax-free and I can deduct the interest."

Home Sweet Home Business

If you have an office in your home, you can take a nice tax deduction. According to NOLO.com, here are the requirements to take your home deduction:

- **Requirement 1.** Regular and exclusive use. You must

regularly use part of your home only for a trade or business.

- **Requirement 2.** Principal place of business. You must also be able to show that you use your home as your main place of business. Or you must be able to show at least one of the following: (1) You meet patients, clients, or customers at home. (2) You use a separate structure on your property exclusively for business.

Be ready to prove to the IRS that you can take the home office deduction. These steps can help establish your legal right to deduct home office expenses:

- Photograph your home office and draw a diagram showing its location in your home. Keep this in your tax folder.
- Have business mail sent to your home.
- Use your home address on business cards, stationery, and in ads.
- Get a separate phone line for the business.
- Have clients or customers visit your home office and log those visits.
- Keep track of the time you spend working at home.

While the home office deduction has benefits, it also includes rules and responsibilities. Remember that whenever you get a tax break, strings are usually attached.

Lord of the Landlords

Should you rent your old home if you move? Here are some advantages to consider:

- Allows you to keep the property along with potential appreciation.
- Tax deductions can offset income generated.
- If you plan to move back to the area, you'll have a place to live.

Now here a few disadvantages:

- Hassles of maintenance or expenses to have someone manage the property.
- If you sell the rental, you can be taxed on the whole profit.
- Potential legal or other liabilities with tenants.
- Potential property repairs and damages.

If you don't plan to return to the home, think twice about keeping the property if it's long distance. However, if you move nearby, you like the home, and it's in a good area for respectable tenants, it could be a good investment and income stream for years.

Helpful resource: National Association of Residential Property Managers <www.narpm.org>.

Reverse It and Release It!

Retirement can be a time to relax, pursue your lifetime dreams, start a new career, or travel. It can also be a complex time: funding health care while preserving the estate for survivors. If you need extra income to enhance your quality of life while remaining in your home, investigate a reverse mortgage.

A reverse mortgage, for homeowners aged 62 and over, provides easy access to home equity they have built over the years. The tax-free equity can be used to purchase long-term care insurance or pay medical costs, which can help protect other assets and savings. Some retirees use the tax-free equity as income to fund life insurance, which can leave a tax-free asset to their survivors.

A reverse mortgage is a lien against the property that must be repaid when the borrower prematurely leaves the property. Upon death, the full value of the property is not included in the estate for tax purposes, because the value of the mortgage reduces the property value. All accrued interest in the reverse mortgage would be available as a tax deduction upon repayment of the loan.

Helpful resource: National Reverse Mortgage Lenders Association <www.reversemortgage.org>. For a free guide call: 1-866-264-4466.

9

Whistle While
You Work

{
Lazy people want much but get little,
but those who work hard will prosper
(Prov. 13:4, NLT).
}

YOU MAY NOT BE FORTUNATE ENOUGH to inherit a large estate or lucky enough to win the lottery. Most people will have to work for money and after living expenses, use what's left to provide income when we can't or don't want to work anymore.

Income is the source of wealth. The higher your income, the higher your chance of building wealth to provide for your lifetime needs and for loved ones. Recent studies show that national income levels are falling and won't get better unless our youth are better educated and trained.

According to the National Center for Public Policy and Higher Education, the proportion of workers with high school diplomas and college degrees will decrease, and the personal income of Americans will decline.

Get Smart!

Solomon said, "If the ax is dull and its edge unsharpened, more strength is needed, but skill will bring success" (Eccles. 10:10).

How can you command a high income or an above average income? It used to be that the harder you worked the more you got paid, but manual labor has an income ceiling, unless you start your own company and hire laborers.

In today's technological world, you must work smarter not just harder. You have to have a competitive edge. Those who gain the education and skill to set them apart from the crowd are indispensable and will command a higher income. Getting that degree or becoming certified—even if it takes you several more years of sacrifice—could be well worth it. This research shows the incomes of various education levels according to the U.S. Census Bureau:

2003 Average Income by Education Level

	Men	Women
Total	$44,726	$28,367
< Ninth Grade	20,724	15,393
> Ninth Grade, No Diploma	21,818	13,767
High School Graduate/Equivalent	33,265	21,659
Some College, No Degree	36,419	22,615
Associate's Degree	43,463	29,538
Bachelor's Degree	63,084	38,448
Master's Degree	76,892	48,205
Professional Degree	136,128	72,444
Doctorate Degree	95,895	73,515

The income difference between the average wage of a bachelor's degree and that of a high school graduate could be as much as $30,000 annually. Over a 30-year period that totals $900,000! It pays to go to school. If you don't have a degree, get one.

When I graduated from high school, college was the furthest thing from my mind. I just wanted to work and party. After a few years I went to college with a major in commercial art while working full time selling insurance. I started making a good income. My work demanded more time, and I never finished my degree. I eventually became securities licensed and certified as a financial planner. Since I'm self-employed, a college degree would have little affect on my income. If I worked for a company and wanted to advance, I would need a degree or certification.

Being in the right place at the right time has much to do with your success. Look for careers that will have a high demand in the marketplace and will require skilled workers.

"Observe people who are good at their work—skilled workers are always in demand and admired; they don't take a back seat to anyone," Solomon said in Prov. 22:29 (TM).

The charts below show a government forecast of the highest job growth areas in the future:

Top Paying Jobs Overall According to Careerbuilder.com
(requiring at least a four-year college degree)

• Physicians and surgeons	$147,000
• Aircraft pilots	133,500
• Chief executives	116,000
• Electrical and electronic engineers	112,000
• Lawyers and judges	99,800
• Dentists	90,000
• Pharmacists	85,500
• Management analysts	84,700
• Computer and information system managers	83,000
• Financial analysts, managers, and advisers	84,000
• Marketing and sales managers	80,000
• Education administrators	80,000

Top 10 Fastest-Growing Occupations from 2002 to 2012
According to Federal Government's Bureau of Labor Statistics

Occupation	Percent Growth
Medical assistants	59
Network systems and data communications analysts	57
Physician assistants	49
Social and human service assistants	49
Home health aides	48
Medical records, health information technicians	47
Physical therapist aides	46
Computer software engineers, applications	46
Computer software engineers, systems software	45
Physical therapist assistants	45

Top Paying Jobs Not Requiring a High School Degree

These jobs tend to require on-the-job training and work experience:

• Industrial production managers	$36,000
• Bailiffs, correctional officers, and jailers	36,400
• Drafters	36,000
• Construction managers	33,600
• Electricians	31,900

Top Paying Jobs for High School Graduates

These occupations emphasize work experience and on-the-job training instead of formal education:

• Computer software engineers	$58,900
• Computer/information systems managers	56,400
• Computer programmers	55,000
• Network systems and data communications analysts	49,000
• General and operations managers	48,000
• Database, network, and computer systems administrators	48,000

Prepare for New Opportunities

"Sow your seed in the morning, and at evening let not your hands be idle, for you do not know which will succeed, whether this or that, or whether both will do equally well" (Eccles. 11:6).

In today's world it helps to diversify your income sources. No longer do we spend our whole careers with one company. With all the corporate downsizing, mergers, and jobs shifting overseas, a person's paycheck could shut off quickly. So finding opportunities to diversify your income is important. Having additional income or a small business to fall back on will help keep you out of debt and on track in meeting your long-term goals.

Developing a hobby or studying a field of interest besides your current career may provide a way to diversify your income and provide tax breaks. Look for ways to make income from your hobby. Learn all about it, but most of all, have fun with it. Starting a small business on the side may provide additional resources to meet obligations, pay down debt, invest, or gift.

However, balancing time between work, family, personal time, and faith activities is a tougher challenge if you add additional work or study. So be careful and prayerful about your time commitment, and remember Solomon's advice, "Do not wear yourself out to get rich; have the wisdom to show restraint" (Prov. 23:4).

I struggle with the thought of working more than one job because it can take time away from family, serving God, and other responsibilities. It's easy to wear yourself out just to raise your standard of living; it may not be worth it. Ask God to show you what steps you should take to increase your income. Seek the advice of a career counselor or a mentor. If you take on another job, it may mean sacrificing spare time and short-term purchases until you get the education or skill necessary to be in the field of your dreams.

I work with a client who is doing that. Tim is in his early 40s and has worked for the U.S. postal service for 15 years. His wife, Claire, also works, and they have one daughter. For 3 years he has gone to college part-time to complete his bachelor's degree so he can be a physician's assistant. He just got accepted into a program.

Tim and Claire have paid cash for his college degree and avoided the temptation to buy better things. They have accumulated $60,000 in the postal retirement savings plan. Their sacrifice is not over, since he will not work during his medical school training. They can do this because they don't have debt and can live within their means.

Whistle at Work

When did you last whistle while doing your work? You should enjoy your work, and it should be satisfying. If you're not happy with your job or occupation, plan to do something you enjoy. Life is too short to spend 30 years dreading work. Your work should be a blessing, something you can look back on and say was worth it.

How can you find the career path or occupation that utilizes your God-given gifts? It all goes back to finding what you're passionate about, what your gifts are, and what you're good at. I strongly recommend reading *Finding the Career That Fits You* written by Ellis/Burkett. This workbook includes personality analysis and skill-assessment exercises. Even if you are already on a career path, taking a skills assessment test could help you find that hobby or other interest to diversify your income potential.

Nothing is wrong with making money and getting ahead. In

fact, the Bible talks about being industrious and working hard and warns against being lazy (see Prov. 10:4). At least 14 verses in Proverbs talk about the negative affects of the "sluggard."

While it's wise to be industrious, it is equally important to balance work and personal time. God worked during the week creating the world, but on the seventh day He kicked back and took it easy. I believe He expects us to do the same—work hard during the week and then set aside a day to worship Him and revive the body (see Exod. 20:9-10).

At times work on Sunday is necessary, but it shouldn't be a way of life. If you're struggling because your job requires you to work on the Sabbath, ask God to show you what to do. Trust Him and leave it in His hands to work out.

What sacrifices are you making to live out your dreams and future goals? Sit down, set some goals, and dream about your future. Then follow through on it. Make sure the sacrifices you make will not only take you to your desired destination but also leave you with no regrets. Developing a written plan and action strategy to meet your goals will take time and effort, but this is the foundation for building a rewarding career. Why not start today?

Remember my friend, Quin Tran—the television journalist who walked away from a successful career to be a better mother? Her family is where her heart is. After struggling with other career options, Quin quit her job. She traded in the Blackberry for more time at the park. She traded in a high salary and perks for priceless hours with her young daughter. It was a bold step and brought financial risks.

Quin started her own consulting business. She's using her talents and years in the media to produce corporate videos, assist with public relations, and help organizations with communication needs. Her business allows her to manage her own time and schedule projects around her child's preschool hours. The unpredictable factor is the amount of money she will earn.

That's where organization skills come into the picture. She and her husband have learned to run their household on a leaner budget. They take fewer vacations and manage money closer, but their financial goals remain the same—monthly dollars are automatically deducted into retirement savings accounts, college funds, life insurance, and charities. Today, Quin is whistling while she works. She enjoys helping others, has the family time she wants, and saves for the future.

"Whatever your hand finds to do, do it with all your might, for in the grave, where you are going, there is neither working nor planning nor knowledge nor wisdom" (Eccles. 9:10).

Self-Evaluation and Action Plan

Is my job satisfying? _____

If not, what can I do to make it more rewarding? _____

_____

What do I need to do to increase my earning potential? __

_____

What occupation would I like to consider as a career or small business opportunity? _____

_____

After reflecting on my working career, if the following things happened, I would be satisfied: _____

_____

What steps can I take to make these things happen? _____

Study Scriptures to Consider for Income and Work

Ecclesiastes 3:15, 22—work is a person's heritage and purpose, a blessing

3:18-19—reward in life, enjoy it

10:10—sharpen your mind, get wisdom

11:6—diversify income

Applying the Parable of the Talents in Your Life's Work

Background reading: Matt. 25:14-30

- **Ability Matters.** How capable and trustworthy are you with your gifts, talents, and money? People who use their ability wisely will be rewarded.
- **God Is Not a "Socialist."** He doesn't hand out to everyone the same. He gives to each according to the person's ability.
- **Hard Work Leads to Promotion.** Many people are afraid of hard work—they don't understand the rewards of a job well done. Those who work hard and do a good job will be rewarded and promoted.
- **Give 100 Percent.** When working on a project, do you give up easily or do you exhaust all the possibilities until it is finished? Giving 100 percent is doing the best you can do at that point and time.
- **Take Calculated Risks.** Sometimes you have to go out on a limb and take a chance. A calculated risk has been studied and planned carefully—it's not haphazard. The higher the risk, the higher the reward.

Other Good Resources for Occupational and Career Planning

- *Do What You Love for the Rest of Your Life: A Practical Guide to Career Change and Personal Renewal* by Bob Griffiths
- www.careerbuilder.com

Train a Child

Solomon said, "Direct your children onto the right path, and when they are older, they will not leave it" (Prov. 22:6, NLT). What parent doesn't want his or her child to be successful in life? Here are a few ideas for teaching your child about money:

- **Involve Your Child in the Family Budget Process.** Let children see where the money goes. As we model good spending and saving habits, they better understand why they can't have everything they want.
- **Give Them an Allowance.** Set guidelines for their allowance. Establish set chores around the house. Make a reasonable list and hold them responsible to complete their tasks. If they are slack in their chores, do not reward them. Challenge them to go the extra mile by having optional jobs they can do to receive a bonus.

  Some parents struggle giving their child an allowance because they think the child's responsibility is to help around the house. While this philosophy has merit, I believe children learn more about money and responsibility as we let them manage an allowance. The key is setting up guidelines and following through with them.
- **Establish a Budget for Their Allowance.** As small as their allowance may seem, help your child create a sim-

ple budget. Create a spirit of generosity in your children by showing them the importance of giving to church and the less fortunate. Putting aside money from each allowance for short-term and long-term savings goals will teach them to plan ahead. Then let them enjoy the rewards of their labor by spending the remaining on whatever they desire.

We use a basic envelope system to allocate their allowance. Get five envelopes and label them:

10 percent	Tithe (Church—the Lord's work)
10 percent	Giving (Directly helping the less fortunate)
20 percent	Short-term Savings (For that special toy or gadget, vacation money, family gifts, etc.)
20 percent	Long-term Savings (For longer-term goals such as their first vehicle, college, or investments)
40 percent	Free Spending Account

- **Set Up a Savings Account.** When your child's short-term savings envelope reaches a certain level, or on a regular schedule (monthly or quarterly), take your child to the bank and put money in a savings account. Also create a file for statements each month. Encourage children to spend this account only on their specific short-term goals.

- **Invest in a Stock Mutual Fund.** When your child's long-term savings account has reached $100, apply for a stock mutual fund account. If the child is younger than 18, you will need to open a custodian officially known as a Uniform Gifts to Minors Act (UGMA) or Uniform Transfer to Minors Act (UTMA), depending on your state laws. This account lets you control the account but is considered the child's money legally. If your child starts to earn income, you can also establish a custodian Roth IRA mutual fund account.

Review the mutual fund annual report and monthly statements with your child, and create a filing system. Encourage your child to use this account for longer-term goals.

I have found that the Young Investor (offered by Columbia Investment Management) offers a great Web site for children and teens <www.younginvestors.com>. The site is also helpful for adults and teachers who want to learn more about investing. Another great Web site is the Mutual Fund Investor's Center <www.mflea.com>.

When you consider your child's or grandchild's future, nothing can help more than a good education. There are many ways to help provide the needed funds for your loved one's higher education. Here are some general funding techniques for education needs:

- **Qualified State Tuition Programs** (Section 529 Plans)

  Authorized under Internal Revenue Code Section 529, these plans let a donor contribute money to a child's account. There are two types of plans: a prepaid tuition plan and a savings plan. Prepaid tuition plans guarantee the investment will pace with increases in the college tuition. Savings plans grow tax-free. Funds withdrawn to pay for education expenses are also free from federal income tax. The child may attend almost any accredited university, college, or trade school. The donor controls the account and can transfer benefits to certain family members without penalty. Withdrawals without penalty are also allowed for scholarship, disability, and death. Pension Protection Act of 2006 removed the 2010 expiration of the 529 tax exemption. This new development should bode well for this much-favored education savings vehicle.

• **Coverdell Education Savings Accounts** (formerly Education IRAs). Deposit up to $2,000 per year into a Coverdell Education Savings Account (ESA) for children younger than 18 years. Anyone can contribute to the Coverdell as long as the total contributions during the year do not exceed $2,000. Amounts deposited grow tax-free, and distributions are tax-free if the child's qualified higher education expenses at an eligible educational institution for the year equal or exceed the amount of withdrawal. Eligible expenses also include elementary and secondary school (K-12) costs and the cost of computer equipment, Internet services, and software.

Amounts withdrawn from a Coverdell ESA that exceed the child's qualified education expense are generally subject to income tax and to an additional 10 percent tax. There are provisions to rollover funds to certain family members' use if the child does not need the money for postsecondary education.

• **Uniform Gifts to Minors Act (UGMA) and Uniform Transfers to Minors Act (UTMA).** With these plans, the donor can make a gift to a custodian account of a minor child. The standard rules regarding gift tax exclusions apply. The donor can contribute a variety of different assets: stocks, bonds, mutual funds, real estate, or cash. The funds can be used for any purpose including education.

Upon reaching legal age (18 or 21), the child has full control over the account to use for any purpose. Taxes are also paid in the year that income or gains are realized and therefore don't have the restrictions the Coverdell ESA and the 529 plans do.

Children do not pay taxes on the first $850 in annual income (2006 figures), due to the standard deduction. Subsequent income is taxed at either the child's rate or the parents' rate: Before a child reaches age 18, the next $850 in income is taxed at the child's rate. Earnings above $1,700 are taxed at the parents' marginal rate. All income (after the first $850) earned by children age 18 and older is taxed at the child's rate. This is often referred to as the kiddie tax.

- **U.S. Savings Bonds.** Interest earned by U.S. Series EE Bonds is free from state income taxes. If the bonds are used for higher education expenses, all or some of the interest may also be tax-free. The bonds must be registered in the parent's name and redeemed in the same year as the eligible tuition and fees are paid.

Resources

Preparing Your Child for College—A Resource Book for Parents <http://www.ed.gov/pubs/Prepare/index.html>

College Funding Solutions, Inc. <www.mycollegeinfo.com>

Financial aid resource <www.FinAid.org>

10

Leaving It Behind

{
Everyone comes naked from their mother's womb,
and as everyone comes, so they depart.
They take nothing from their toil that they
can carry in their hands *(Eccles. 5:15, TNIV)*.
}

ANNA NICOLE SMITH, former entertainer, died on February 8, 2007, at the age of 39. Smith was the widow of Texas oil tycoon J. Howard Marshall II. Smith married Marshall in 1994, when he was 89. His estate was estimated at $500 million in 1995.

Marshall's family has disputed Smith's claim to his estate. Anna Nicole Smith signed her will on July 30, 2001, directing her estate to go to her only child, Daniel. A few days after Anna's daughter, Danielynn, was born, Daniel died. Smith's will did not provide contingencies for other children.

Because of Smith's poorly drafted will, the courts fought over her burial and the custody of her daughter. Her body was finally laid to rest three weeks after her death, but the settlement of her estate could take years to resolve. Her example of poor estate planning provides law professors with many years of teaching material!

You would think wealthy individuals would take more time to plan and minimize the costs of dying, but just because you have wealth doesn't mean you know how to handle it. Even the wealthy need advice to preserve and pass on their estates. In fact, the more wealth you have, the more you have to work to preserve it from taxes and potential lawsuits. If you have a large estate, upon your death as much as 46 percent of your total estate could go to taxes.

Not having an estate plan is one of the biggest deficits in planning I see. Could it be that people don't plan for distribution of their estate because they don't think they will die? Is it because they don't want to think about dying? Or, is it because they don't care?

You know you will pass from this life at some point, you just don't know when. And you know you can't take it with you. So why not record how you want your affairs to be handled? If you don't, your estate may be squandered away. If you have young children or others depending upon you, it's even more important to plan for their care.

Most people want to leave something for their loved ones and church, community, or other causes. Wisdom says, "A good man leaves an inheritance for his children's children, but a sinner's wealth is stored up for the righteous" (Prov. 13:22).

An estimated 4 out of 10 people have a will or written estate plan. The estate planning process can be complicated because everybody is different and has unique wishes. Not only that, you also have to weave your planning around specific state and federal laws.

Here are basic ways you can pass on your estate:

- Do nothing—no plan
- Title property and assets in joint tenancy
- Through a will
- Through a trust

If you die without a will or trust, you die intestate, which are your state's statutes on settling an estate for those who don't have a plan. When death occurs, title to the deceased's property and assets has to be transferred to the intended heirs. If the court has no instructions to follow, it must pass according to the state statutes—the laws of intestacy.

So if you don't have a plan, your state has one for you—and it may not be what you would have intended. All property and assets titled in your name will be settled in court proceedings known as probate. The probate judge will follow the laws of intestacy to determine who gets your stuff.

If you are married, most states award the surviving spouse all of it. However, if you are married with children, the surviving spouse may get half of the estate, with the rest divided among the children.

If the children are minors, the court must appoint a guardian, typically the surviving parent, and a custodian for their share of the estate (which can also be the surviving parent). Even if the surviving parent is the guardian and custodian of the child's share, he or she must report to the courts on how the funds are used on the child's behalf.

If you die as a single parent of minor children, who will take care of them? If you don't have a plan, the courts will decide who takes care of your children and their inheritance. If you have a blended family, things could get even more complicated.

Dying without a plan has no benefit: You throw your estate and survivors' future at the courts. You subject your estate to costly proceedings. Your heirs are at the court's mercy. Establish a written, legal document that outlines your wishes and desires, or leave it to chance and the courts.

Probate is the court process that occurs after a person dies and carries out the terms of his or her will. When a person dies having only a will, a probate proceeding is usually required to administer his or her estate. Not having a will also requires a probate proceeding.

Disadvantages of Probate

Probate can be lengthy—from six months to two years or longer. Probate can be costly and inconvenient, running from 2 to 8 percent of the total value of your estate, depending on the circumstances and state statutes.

Probate is public. Once filed in the probate action, your will and any other information filed in the probate action generally become public records.

Joint title is the popular choice of holding property or assets between married couples. I have also seen this done between elderly parents and their children. Holding property in joint tenancy will avoid probate and pass it directly to the surviving tenants.

However, many things can go wrong with holding property in joint tenancy. For example, if joint owners die simultaneously, there are no survivors for the property to pass to. The property will then be distributed to the deceased's last will and testament; if they don't have one, the scenario from dying without a plan (dying intestate) will kick in.

Holding property jointly with someone who is not a spouse can cause problems. Here are potential dangers of titling property with others than your spouse:

The property or asset could be subject to garnishment or claimed in the event that the joint tenant holder is divorced or sued for liability damages. Also, when you add someone other than your spouse to a piece of property, this could be considered a gift for tax purposes (current annual limit on gift to an individual without being subject to gift taxes is $12,000).

Jointly held property also passes by title, outside of the will. So, no matter what your will says, jointly held property will pass to the surviving tenant or to whomever is listed on the title.

In summary, jointly held property is OK only between spouses—even at that it is only a temporary fix, because upon the first death, the survivor is then the sole owner of the property and eventually it will be subject to probate.

When in the case of an elderly parent, at the least, the child should be appointed as attorney in fact using a durable power of attorney. The account could be set up as a payable-on-death or a beneficiary-designated account listing the child as beneficiary upon death. Most banks and financial institutions provide for this type of account. Using these methods will avoid a death probate and guardianship in the event of incapacity by using the durable power of attorney. It will also keep assets in the parent's name while living and avoid any gift tax issues or other problems that could arise with jointly held property.

If you wish to reduce the cost and time of probate, consider an alternative method of estate planning—a living trust. A living trust is a private document that allows your estate to be settled by those you appoint to do so, without having to go to court. These are not just for the wealthy. If you own title to property and various accounts, consider a living trust.

Many living trusts are revocable as long as you are alive. Once your trust has been established, you transfer title to your property and accounts in the name of your trust. You don't own any more assets in your name—they are now owned by your trust. You can list yourself as the trustee (manager) and as the beneficiary. You (or you and your spouse) have complete control while you are alive. When you die, there are no assets titled in your name, so your property and assets are settled by those named as successor trustees, avoiding the probate process.

I have seen this process work many times. For years I have helped clients set up trusts. Several of those clients have passed away. Those who established their trusts and funded them with all eligible property and accounts (excluding IRAs and retirement plans) have avoided probate and have settled their estates in a private, timely manner.

One of the biggest issues you must decide is who will be your successor trustee upon your death. You must choose someone who can notify beneficiaries, complete paperwork, and keep records—preferably someone with business sense. You can list more than one person to serve, but more than one or two could be problematic, especially if all have to sign off on documents.

One of my clients was a single parent who listed all five of her children as successor trustees. All of the children lived in different states, so each document that needed signing had to be mailed to one beneficiary, and then forwarded to the next, and so on, until each child signed.

It would make more sense to name only one child, who may live closer, to be the first successor death trustee and then the rest as backups. Even with all of the children listed as successor trustees, the estate was settled and distributed within 90 days, completely avoiding probate.

Often, I have helped clients who did not have anyone qualified to be their successor trustee. In this case you can list a corporate trustee (i.e., trust department) to handle the affairs of settling the trust. You can also list a corporate trustee to help a child or other family member in the process. Even paying a corporate trustee to carry out your wishes and handle your affairs could be much cheaper, save time, and avoid the public display of the probate process. The cost to establish a trust may be higher than a will; however, it could be worth the investment.

The key to having a living trust is keeping it funded. I once met with a retired couple who brought in their documents for a review. They were proud they had established a living trust. After reviewing the document and all of the titles to their accounts and property, I realized their trust was not listed as the owner on any of their stuff. Their trust was a shell and owned nothing. The attorney who prepared the document had listed a memorandum of property, which listed most of their property when they established the trust.

Had the clients died, their estate would have gone through the probate process. Their property would have ended up in the trust for final distribution because there was a pour-over-will executed. The pour-over-will provides that any property listed outside the trust be transferred into it by way of the probate process (just like a regular will). So, if you establish a living trust, keep your eligible property titled in the name of your trust. Ineligible property usually is confined to IRAs and retirement plans.

It doesn't matter how large or small your estate. The type of property you own is important. For example, if you are married and own several pieces of property, a house, and several brokerage accounts, you could pass almost everything to your surviving spouse using joint-tenancy titled property, but the surviving spouse would then have to make plans for the property to pass on to whomever he or she wants upon his or her death. So, it is a temporary solution.

Many times people ask what to do if a single person has very little—say, a house and a bank account—and doesn't have the funds to establish a living trust. What options does this person have to pass his or her property directly to the heirs? As mentioned earlier, I don't recommend jointly held property between nonmarried people. So, here are a few other ways to directly pass accounts or property to intended heirs:

A qualified personal residence trust (QPRT). The home owner, the grantor, places his or her personal residence into the irrevocable trust that lets him or her retain possession or use for a specified term, generally 10 to 20 years. At the end of this term, the personal residence passes to the trust beneficiaries.

At that point if the grantor wishes to live in the house, the grantor must pay market value rent to the trustee or the beneficiaries of the trust. Grantors can reduce their potential estate tax liability by transferring assets to a QPRT, because it is not included in their estate unless they die before the QPRT termination. The gift of the residence is subject to the federal gift tax amounts.

The QPRT can be a valuable tool to transfer residence for the benefit of the children and possibly help reduce any estate taxes from the grantor's estate.

Payable upon death (POD) or beneficiary designations (as mentioned above) for bank accounts, brokerage accounts, and mutual fund accounts can be established that list who the account will pass to upon the owner's death. If you are single, always ask if this is an option on the account you are establishing and name those you would like to receive your account.

Property or assets that automatically bypass the will and (avoid) the probate process:

- Jointly held property (joint tenancy with rights of survivor, most common between spouses)
- Life insurance policies with a direct beneficiary listed; also contingent beneficiaries are important
- Retirement plans—IRAs, 401(k)s, etc.—that have designated beneficiaries

If you have a retirement plan and are married, your spouse is usually the best choice as your primary beneficiary. Surviving spouses have special privileges when inheriting a retirement plan. They can roll it over into a spousal IRA and defer income taxes until their required distribution date at age 70½.

Listing your children as secondary or contingent beneficiaries is usually advised unless your child has special needs and is receiving Social Security benefits. Leaving an inheritance to this child could jeopardize his or her eligibility to continue receiving financial support. If so, establish a special needs trust for that child's inheritance.

If you have no beneficiaries, or don't know who to list, don't list your estate as beneficiary. Listing your estate will guarantee the account or policy will be subject to the probate courts. If you have no one to leave your retirement plan or insurance policy to, consider leaving it to your church or other charitable organization. It will go directly to the organization without administrative costs. It will also reduce your taxable estate by the amount you give to the charity.

The primary purpose of an estate plan is to carry out your goals and wishes. A good estate plan identifies the people who are important to you and your plans to care for them during your lifetime and after your death. Estate planning is the process of organizing your affairs for the convenience of your family and loved ones.

Here is a checklist to ask yourself:

- Do I need a will? Or, do I need a trust?
- How can I make things easier for my family if I die or am incapacitated?
- How can I guarantee that those I want to receive my property will actually receive it?
- How can I avoid probate?
- How can I avoid or minimize estate taxes?
- What plans do I need to make for the care of my children in case of my death or incapacity? Who do I want as guardians for my children?
- Who will make personal and medical decisions for me if I can't?
- Who will take care of my property and affairs if I can't?
- Is the estate plan I have now the right one for me?
- What will happen to my business if I die or become disabled?

Leaving Your Legacy

Taking care of dependents and loved ones upon your death may be an important goal, but what about helping the organizations you care about? Have you considered tithing your estate upon death? Here are some strategies to consider:

- Outright gift or testamentary gift
- Gifting of life insurance or retirement funds
- Charitable gift annuity
- Charitable trusts
- Charitable gift funds

One of the lowest-cost methods is an outright gift of property or money. That requires no expensive legal documents and no ongoing administrative expenses. It is a gift with no strings attached, free of any provisions that accompany other gifting strategies. The government needs charities to help meet the needs of society and will give tax deductions to donors if they meet certain guidelines.

Charitable gift annuities are best for older people who need income. This is basically how the gift annuity works: A person wants to make a gift to a charity but needs income for life. He or she deposits $10,000 into the annuity, which pays him or her a lifetime income. Upon death, the rest of the annuity value goes to the charity. The donor gets a tax deduction for the gift and receives a portion of the income as a return of principal free of taxation. At death the value of the annuity is not included in the deceased's estate for tax purposes.

Charitable trusts come in different types. They are typically used when the donor contributes highly appreciated property or other assets. The benefit of the charitable trust is that a highly appreciated investment can be placed in the trust, then sold and capital gain taxes are avoided, leaving more assets to the donor or to the charity. With a charitable lead trust, income from the trust is paid to the charity, and upon the donor's death, the remainder is returned to the estate. With a charitable remainder trust, income from the trust is paid to the donor (and spouse). Upon the donors' deaths the rest of the corpus goes to the charity.

You should consider a charitable trust if you have a piece of property or an investment with substantial appreciation and want to avoid taxes when it is sold. If you need the income from the investment, then consider the charitable remainder trust.

If income is not an objective and you want your heirs to receive the rest, consider the charitable lead trust. The value of the charitable trust is not included in your estate upon your death, so heirs avoid estate taxes.

In some situations you should have your estate plan reviewed, says attorney Forrest J. Danley. Here are examples:

- When you get married
- When you become a parent
- When you reach midlife
- When you move to another state
- At the death, birth, or divorce of children, heirs, beneficiaries, guardians, agents, personal representatives, or trustees
- After a divorce
- Before you remarry (for example, a premarital agreement is often essential)
- When you retire
- When a spouse dies

- If you receive an inheritance or your assets grow significantly

Avoiding Death Taxes

Estate taxes are paid after your death from your estate, depending upon its size. Your state may have an estate tax besides the federal estate tax. If you have any significant amount of wealth, you can save thousands of dollars with some basic estate tax planning. (Remember, your taxable estate can include life insurance proceeds and retirement plan benefits.)

Under the Economic Growth and Tax Reconciliation Act of 2001 (EGTRA 2001), the federal estate tax exemption will continue to increase until it reaches a maximum of $3.5 million applicable in 2009.

Basically, if an individual were to die in 2007 or 2008, he or she would receive a Unified Credit of $780,800, which is the applicable exclusion amount on an estate of $2,000,000. This is the amount an individual can pass on estate tax free. A married person can pass unlimited amounts to the spouse with no estate tax; this is called the unlimited marital deduction. However, upon the death of the surviving spouse, any amounts over the exemption level would be subject to the estate tax.

Some states also have an estate tax or death tax, with exemption amounts lower than the federal amounts. In 2009 the unified credit amount increases to $1,445,800, and the applicable exclusion amount is $3,500,000. In 2010, there is no federal estate tax, but in 2011 it reverts back to a $1,000,000 exclusion amount.

So here is the application: If you are single and your estate is valued close to $2,000,000 and higher, you need to do some planning to minimize or avoid the taxes on your estate (especially after 2010). If you are married and your estate exceeds $2,000,000, you should consider the unified credit shelter bypass trust that applies to married couples. This planning tool is one of the most used ways to reduce estate taxes.

Remember the rate of the estate tax starts at 46 percent for any amounts over the exemption. So plan your estate with this in mind.

Application

If you are of legal age, you should have the following estate planning documents in place:

- **A Will.** The will should list a representative who will handle the settlement of your estate. You will also want to list guardians for children and how you want your estate distributed.

- **Durable General Power of Attorney for Property.** This document names an agent to make decisions for you and sign on your behalf concerning your assets. If you become incapacitated, the agent can still do those things if the document is drafted to be durable.

- **Durable Power of Attorney for Health Care.** This document lets an agent make your personal and medical care decisions if you can't make them yourself. It is also durable, to be effective if you become incapacitated.

- **Advanced Directive for Health Care.** Under your state laws, this document contains a living will and a health care proxy designation. This will let you determine the level of care you want and level of life support you desire in the event of a terminal illness.

If you have substantial assets or many pieces of titled property, consider some of the more advanced estate planning tools in lieu of or in addition to a will:

- **A Revocable Living Trust.** This private document takes the place of a will. If it is properly funded with all of your assets, you can avoid the probate process and have your estate settled in private and more efficiently pass to your heirs.

- **A Credit Shelter Bypass Trust.** This trust is designed to help avoid estate taxes upon the second spouse's death. Upon your death, instead of passing your estate directly to your spouse, you can place the federal exemption equivalent amount (up to $2,000,000 in 2007) in your bypass trust. Your surviving spouse can use the income from your bypass trust, and upon your spouse's death it is distributed to heirs and avoids the federal estate tax. (Had you passed all of your estate to your spouse directly, upon his or her death only $2,000,000 would have been exempt from taxes.) Using this tool, a married couple could avoid taxes on a $4,000,000 estate.

- **A Life Insurance Trust.** Did you know your life insurance policy death benefits avoid income taxes to your beneficiaries, but your policies are included as part of your taxable estate, so consider having them owned by an irrevocable life insurance trust (ILIT) that you create. The ILIT lets the insurance policy pass to the heirs without estate taxes. Premiums on the policy are paid with annual gifts to the ILIT, which the beneficiaries of the ILIT disclaim. The proceeds avoid the estate tax because there are no incidents of ownership of the insured.

- **Annual Gift Tax Exclusion.** This exclusion allows you to make gifts to as many people as you want as long as each gift does not exceed $12,000 (2006, indexed annually for inflation). This can be an effective way to reduce your taxable estate and let heirs and loved ones benefit from your gifts instead of waiting to give it all to them at your death. You can make gifts in cash or other property, but remember, if you gift highly appreciated property or stocks, your cost basis will transfer to the new owner, resulting in a higher tax liability when he or she sells it.

An attorney called me one day and said he had a client whose husband had just been killed and left his wife and small children $1,000,000 in life insurance benefits. The attorney was concerned the wife would blow the money before he could help her get it into a trust to provide for her long-term needs.

Before the attorney got the trust drawn, the wife bought a home, a new Corvette, and went on a spending spree to Las Vegas. In two weeks she spent $400,000. We put $600,000 into a trust for her and the children's benefit, but that didn't last long. Her new boyfriend talked her into investing the funds into a risky start-up business venture. What a waste.

Many times people who aren't used to having money will quickly go through any they get. The husband could have done several things to protect the estate. He could have created spendthrift clauses or provisions for part of the proceeds to be paid in monthly installments.

Many times I see minor children listed as beneficiaries of large life insurance policies with no special provisions, instructions, or strings attached. Even some adult children could use guidance. Would you write a check today for $500,000 and just give it to your child and say, "Here's some money; do whatever you want"?

Why do basically the same thing with a life insurance policy? You can also have your life insurance proceeds paid into a trust, so you can dictate how they will receive their benefits and can protect their inheritance from creditors. If the proceeds are large, you may want to have part of their benefits paid in a monthly lifetime check. This way they can't spend it all at once and may gain wisdom on how to handle their inheritance. You can have this income stream created through an income annuity, which can be paid over a certain term.

Taking care of your estate planning will give you peace of mind that your affairs are in order and your wishes are carried out. You may not be able to take it with you, but you can plan as though you were still involved in your heirs' lives.

As you journey through life, also think about the values you want to pass on to the next generation. What experiences and bits of wisdom do you want to communicate to the generations to come?

In days of old, stories were passed down through the generations, and family legacies were kept alive. Telling stories is one way to pass on key aspects of your legacy, but stories can be distorted.

With recent technology, such as digital videos, you can tell your story as you want it to be preserved. My pastor, Mark Hollingsworth, is doing that with his brothers Stan and Terry Toler.

All three brothers are ministers in the Church of the Nazarene and live around Oklahoma City with their families. They are creating a DVD in which they tell their family's history with pictures, music Terry has written, and the important stories of their lives and families—the convictions and character qualities they want to pass on to their children and grandchildren. They are also putting together a book with more stories and photos.

What legacy will you pass on to your heirs? Preserving your values and life stories on paper or video for the next generation is a great way to leave a legacy.

Self-Evaluation

Upon my death I want to leave my possessions to _____

_____

What instructions do I want to leave my heirs on handling any wealth I pass on? _____

_____

Do I have special instructions for certain heirs; does their inheritance need protection? _____

_____

How do I want to benefit my church or other charities? Do I have special instructions for them? _____

_____

Who do I trust to help settle my estate and administer ongoing provisions? Who would be my second choice, a backup? _____

_____

Does my current estate plan need reviewing? Have any changes in my personal circumstances, business, or estate laws merit any changes in my plan? _____

Do I have my funeral, burial, and memorial service preferences arranged and communicated in writing? _____

Will my heirs or executor of my estate be able to locate important documents upon my death? How can I make my instructions easily accessible to my heirs? _____

Who can help me get my estate plans in order? Who have my friends or other advisers used? _____

Good people leave an inheritance for their children's children,
but a sinner's wealth is stored up for the righteous
(*Prov. 13:22, TNIV*).

Suggested Reading

The American Bar Association Guide to Wills and Estates, Second Edition: Everything You Need to Know About Wills, Estates, Trusts, and Taxes

Beyond the Grave: The Right Way and the Wrong Way of Leaving Money to Your Children (and Others), Revised Edition, by Gerald M. Condon, ESQ, and Jeffrey L. Condon, ESQ

Family Wealth: Keeping It in the Family: How Family Members and Their Advisers Preserve Human, Intellectual, and Financial Assets for Generations, by James E. Hughes Jr.

11

Seeking Counsel

{ Plans fail for lack of counsel,
but with many advisers they succeed
(Prov. 15:22). }

PROFESSIONAL ATHLETES have coaches to help them in
every aspect of their game. These coaches have years of experience and wisdom and help their clients stretch their minds
and physical abilities. A capable trainer can help an individual
accomplish more and increase the odds of reaching goals. Successful people surround themselves with advisers and mentors
that have track records of success.

The same concept applies in your life—whether it concerns your business, personal, or spiritual goals. Tapping into
the knowledge of a seasoned adviser can put you years ahead
in working toward your life goals.

When seeking a personal coach or adviser, keep in mind
this foundational step: Does the adviser's philosophy line up
with your values and foundational belief system? Taking advice
from someone who doesn't share a similar belief system could

be costly. Many life coaches offer programs for finding success based strictly upon self-help and help from spiritual guides. Many of these programs offer basic ideas that can be used; however, advisers who fail to recognize where true wisdom comes from can lead you away from true fulfillment and peace.

In Prov. 2:6, King Solomon said, "All wisdom comes from the LORD, and so do common sense and understanding" (CEV). Also, 3:19 says, "By his wisdom and knowledge the LORD created heaven and earth" (CEV).

Who would you rather get advice from on life matters? Some guru or some spiritual guide to help find your inner child? Or, would you rather get it from the Source of life that created you and has a purpose just for you? This wisdom is greater than any other plan, "Wisdom is supreme; therefore get wisdom. Though it cost all you have, get understanding" (4:7). So when looking for a coach, look for one who knows the true source of wisdom and has the experience and knowledge to apply it in your situation.

Look to the Bible as your first source for direction. When was the last time you read Proverbs and Ecclesiastes? These books reveal much of Solomon's experiences in interacting with others, handling money, avoiding pitfalls, and benefits of leading a practical and balanced life.

Solomon started out by asking the Source of wisdom to bless him. When we acknowledge our limitations and ask for help, this opens the door for wisdom to enter our lives. "If any of you need wisdom, ask God for it. He will give it to you. God gives freely to everyone. He doesn't find fault" (James 1:5, NIRV). Just like Solomon, you can experience this wisdom by asking for help.

The second part to this principle is that you must expect to receive it, "But when you ask, you must believe. You must not doubt. People who doubt are like waves of the sea. The wind blows and tosses them around" (James 1:6, NIRV).

Seeking Financial Advice

It seems everywhere you turn ads, pop-ups, junk e-mails, and investment newsletters entice you to buy their advice or use their products. With all of these financial sources, how do you choose what is best for you?

Occasionally I get invitations to financial workshops that tout the latest method to invest in the stock market. Usually the event is free, but once you get there you find to learn their secret or system you have to spend thousands of dollars.

Most people know they need help. They hear some packaged deal and think it will solve their financial problems. I'm not saying all of these programs are bad, but many times people look for something quick and easy and won't put in the effort to make it work. What they really need is good financial advice specific to their circumstances and a plan to implement it.

The financial world is so complex with tax laws and economic conditions. Unless you are immersed in it daily, it's hard to know everything about investments, taxes, estate, insurance, retirement issues, and how they apply to you.

Whether you are just starting to invest and plan for the future or if you are in retirement, you need a guide to help you make the right financial decisions. We've already seen the effects of procrastination, and the results a bad investment can have on your future. Too many mistakes could hinder your achieving your dreams and goals.

Don't get me wrong, coaches and advisers aren't perfect, and any plan might miss the mark. However, seeking wisdom from those who have experience can help you improve your chances of success.

You can find many types of advisers: insurance agents, stockbrokers, tax professionals, lawyers, and financial planners, as well as specialists in subcategories of these. Many advisers in sales hold themselves out as providing financial planning advice. For example, with the emerging need of financial services, the insurance industry now has all types of investment products for their clients. Many tax advisers and lawyers also offer investments, insurance, and programs to provide their clients with services that used to be outsourced to specialists.

Having a one-stop shop for financial services may be convenient but may not provide objective advice. When you see blended practices or advisers that offer everything, this may be a sign they are too busy trying to do everything for everybody.

Many well-intentioned advisers offer good products and provide value-added service to their clients. Many times this is a good place for a person to start an investment plan or to meet insurance needs. However, if you have already created an investment plan and need advice, you need a financial adviser who can give objective advice and a plan to help you work more efficiently toward your goals.

As you look for a financial adviser, here are a few considerations:

- **Experience.** How many years has the adviser been in practice? What is his or her educational and business background? You need an adviser with at least 5 to 10 years of advising experience. With at least 5 years in the business, he or she should have a decent practice and have passed the point of starving. If you choose someone with less than 5 years, make sure the adviser has a mentor or partner with more experience. Ask about their qualifications. Are they certified in a financial course of study? Having a securities license or a college degree does not qualify an adviser. Their course of study and previous work can tell you a lot.

- **Expertise.** What does the adviser specialize in? What licenses and certifications does he or she hold? Know what services the adviser can and can't provide. The type of adviser you choose will depend on your planning needs. For example, if you need help managing a $500,000 retirement plan rollover, you probably won't drop in at your local insurance agent and leave them your check. You'll probably end up with one of the insurance company's annuity or mutual funds.

I'm not saying your insurance agent isn't competent or that annuities and mutual funds don't have their place in a portfolio, but if you want objective advice on investing life savings without getting locked into a program with severe penalties, choose a trained investment adviser.

If you need a coordinated financial plan that addresses your overall goals, a fee-based adviser such as a certified financial planner or certified public accountant can provide recommendations. But remember, just because someone has a certification doesn't mean he or she is qualified to put a plan together and recommend proven strategies.

Most financial people call themselves financial planners or financial advisers. Dig deeper and find out what's behind the title. Ask them to show you a sample financial plan. Also ask how they will develop your plan. Advisers should be able to provide you with a financial planning process that spells out steps to complete your plan. If the person isn't organized enough to show you a sample plan, go to the next interview.

- **Method of Compensation.** How is the adviser compensated? It's important to know how the adviser makes his or her living and if he or she has conflicts of interest in giving advice. You pay an adviser in one of two ways: commissions or fee-based.

  Commission-only advisers have to sell you something to receive income. This is not bad, as long as you know what's at stake, but it could leave the door open to the temptation of a big payout for the adviser.

  Most insurance agents and some planners have to sell their company's offerings to receive compensation. The adviser has to be insurance licensed or securities licensed to receive commissions from the annuity or a mutual fund company. Nothing is imprudent about an adviser making a commission as long as he or she discloses fees. If you do pay commissions, ask the adviser to show you how it is in your best interest and how the product or service is comparable to others.

  Fee-based advisers receive compensation in one of two methods. One is a flat or hourly rate; and the other is a percentage of assets. If you need an adviser to prepare a financial plan or give you advice in a certain area, you'll typically be charged an hourly rate (from $50 to $200 or more) for his or her services. I suggest the adviser give you a fee range or a cap on the amount he or she will charge.

Advisory fees based on a percentage of assets typically involve portfolio management. These fees will vary depending on the portfolio size and the type of investments. Advisory fees will typically range from 2.5 percent to 1 percent annually. When you enter advisory agreements, you should receive a quarterly report and analysis, along with ongoing management of the portfolio. You should also receive an investment policy statement that outlines your objective and procedures on how your account will be managed.

Ask the adviser for historical returns on similar portfolios. Compare these to industry benchmarks such as the S&P 500 Index, but don't expect to outperform a stock index benchmark if you have fixed income (bonds) in your portfolio mix.

Any time you pay an advisory fee you must receive the firm's ADV Part II and disclosures. You should also sign an advisory agreement that spells out what services the adviser will provide and what fees you will pay. During your initial interview, ask the adviser to provide you with a copy of the ADV Part II schedule and a copy of the advisory agreement.

Does the Adviser Have Support in Place?

Having a large company or affiliated relationships can provide a backup of support for the adviser. However, it may also mean the adviser has loyalty to the company's products whether or not they're the best choice. Always ask the adviser if he or she is a captive representative of a company or affiliated with a financial services firm that may have to sell quotas.

An independent adviser has advantages and disadvantages. More advisers are leaving big securities firms and setting up independent shops. However, some advisers are not cut out to work for themselves and by themselves.

Ask who will assist the adviser with implementing and servicing your plan or accounts. The services you receive may only be as good as the adviser's staff. If the adviser has any kind of practice, he or she will have too much to do keeping up with the stock markets, the tax laws, and servicing accounts. Ask to meet the adviser's staff and ask who is responsible for what duties. If the adviser doesn't have a good support staff, look elsewhere. You must be comfortable with the staff and operations—after all, they'll handle your affairs and money.

Who Does the Adviser Serve?

Know what type of clientele the adviser serves. If you are retired and need help setting up a required distribution from your IRA and want to set up beneficiary provisions that will let your children and grandchildren stretch out the account, you need an adviser who has dealt with estate planning issues.

What Is the Adviser's Philosophy?

Ask an adviser what money means to him or her. When you meet with an adviser, he or she is interviewing for the job of working for you. A seasoned adviser will also wonder, "Is this a client I want to work with?"

Ask the adviser how he or she views the adviser/client relationship. Ask to see the firm's mission statement. If the advisers have a mission statement, you know they have put much thought into their practices and services. And observe the adviser. If he or she does all the talking (goes on about how big and good his or her company is), and doesn't ask you about your philosophy of money and life goals, that adviser probably won't have your best interests in mind because he or she won't even know what those are!

Here is a brief summary of some professional designations in the financial planning and services industry:

- **Certified Financial Planner (CFP).** These advisers know key areas of financial planning, including: tax, estate, insurance, investments, retirement, and the planning process. This is probably the most recognized designation and is not easy to obtain. For more information go to <http://www.cfp.net>.

- **Chartered Financial Consultant (ChFC).** These advisers must complete several years of testing in key areas similar to the CFP. The ChFC designation is a cousin to the Chartered Life Underwriter (CLU) designation, which started with the insurance industry.

- **Certified Public Accountant (CPA).** The CPA's specialty is tax issues. This person must have an accounting degree, a 150-semester-hour credit requirement, and have passed a four-part exam. CPAs can obtain a personal financial specialist (PFS) designation if they focus on financial planning. They must have 250 hours of annual experience in financial planning and pass an additional exam.

Many professional designations are specialized in a particular area, like the chartered financial analyst (CFA), which has extensive course study requirements. Some of the designations may require only a few days of study and a final exam. Check out the designations of an adviser at <http://apps.nasd.com/ datadirectory/nasd/prodesignations.aspx>.

We plan the way we want to live, but only GOD
makes us able to live it *(Prov. 16:9, TM)*.

12
Final Thoughts

Everything has now been heard. And here's the final thing I want to say. Have respect for God and obey his commandments. That's what everyone should do. God will judge everything people do. That includes everything they try to hide. He'll judge everything, whether it's good or evil *(Eccles. 12:13-14, NIRV)*.

THROUGHOUT HIS WRITINGS, Solomon shares many of his life adventures and gives us practical instruction about life, work, money, relationships, and enjoying the fruits of our labor. But he concludes it with an unsympathetic, cut-through-the-chase piece of advice: Revere God and do what His Word says. And remember, you will give an account of your life here on earth.

When you think about being a good steward of your life and the resources you've been given, review the parable of the talents that Jesus shared with His disciples. It is found in Matt. 25:14-30. This parable gives a strong message on the importance of accepting the responsibilities that have been entrusted to us. After reading this passage of scripture, ask yourself these questions:

- What is the clear message of this parable?
- How does this parable relate to me and my finances?
- What are the "talents" or responsibilities I have been entrusted with?
- What steps must I take to increase my "talents" as I work diligently for the causes of Christ?

7 RULES FOR BUILDING WISDOM AND WEALTH

1. **Live on Less than You Make.** *Know where your money is going and control your spending.*

2. **When You Start Earning, Start Saving.** *Build and maintain a cushion or emergency fund, then begin investing in assets than will appreciate. Set aside some liquid cash for investment opportunities.*

3. **Avoid Consumer Debt.** *Pay cash for items you need. Borrow money only for things that appreciate in value, and pay them off early.*

4. **Honor God with the Wealth and Income He Has Provided You.** *Make tithing a regular part of your worship. Give generously to those in need.*

5. **Diversify Your Investments.** *Not just different types of mutual funds, but include real estate, commodities, and other hard assets.*

6. **Insure Against Risk.** *Use insurance and other tools to protect your wealth and your family against death, taxes, and other risks that pose a threat to your financial freedom.*

7. **Leave a Legacy.** *Keep an up-to-date estate plan to accomplish an efficient transfer of wealth to your heirs and a generous gift to charities you cherish.*

Notes

Chapter 1

1. Richard Layard, *Happiness: Lessons from a New Science,* (New York: The Penguin Press, 2005).

2. Richard J. Foster, *Money, Sex, and Power: The Challenge of the Disciplined Life* (New York: Harper Collins, 1985), 24-5.

Chapter 2

1. Julia McCord, article in *Omaha World Herald* (April 23, 2000).

Chapter 3

1. Thomas J. Stanley and William P. Danko, *The Millionaire Next Door: The Surprising Secrets of America's Wealthy* (New York: Simon & Schuster Pocket Books, 1996), 27-69; 211-245.

Chapter 4

1. Anya Kamenetz, *Generation Debt: Why Now Is a Terrible Time to Be Young* (New York: Riverhead Books, 2005), 5-7.

Chapter 7

1. Jeremy J. Siegel, *The Future for Investors: Why the Tried and the True Triumph Over the Bold and New* (New York: Crown Business, 2005), 180-184.